DOING WELL BY DOING GOOD

Praise for *Doing Well by Doing Good*

Church leaders, anxious about the viability of their parishes and congregations in post-Christendom North America, too often turn inward, seeking church-centered means of survival. In this well-written, data-based study grounded in real-life examples, Brendan J. Barnicle conclusively demonstrates that participating in God's mission through local economic enterprises offers a hope-filled future for congregations. Read this book and be inspired to participate in the *missio Dei* in your neighborhood in new and exciting ways!

—**Ian T. Douglas**, retired bishop of the Episcopal Church in Connecticut and former professor of mission and world Christianity at Episcopal Divinity School

Written with practical theological insights and a deep knowledge of congregational leadership, *Doing Well by Doing Good* demonstrates how church-based economic ministries can revitalize local communities and lead practitioners into a deeper understanding of mission for the twenty-first century. Barnicle's study furthers the conversation regarding the need to empower the vocations of all, both inside congregations and in our wider communities, to offer the gifts and resources of the church for the common good. Rather than rehashing traditional models of church growth, this book introduces imaginative and transformational examples of active participation in God's mission through social justice and economic sustainability, which also increases local agency and membership.

—**Sheryl A. Kujawa-Holbrook**, professor of practical theology and Christian histories, Claremont School of Theology; historiographer of The Episcopal Church; editor in chief, *Anglican and Episcopal History*

Brendan J. Barnicle presents a sweeping academic case for the missional (and financial!) benefits of church-based economic enterprises. Grounded in practical theology, Barnicle's book helps congregation leaders see ways in which these enterprises are rooted in and expand God's mission in the world. His in-depth case studies of four congregations bring us inside their stories to see how these enterprises center mission and not money, require deep community discernment, and rely on an interplay of clergy and active lay leadership. This will be a great book for clergy and lay leaders alike who are skeptical of churches starting and/or incubating businesses.

—**Grace Duddy Pomroy**, director, Stewardship Leaders Program at Luther Seminary, and author of *Funding Forward: A Pathway to More Sustainable Models for Ministry*

Doing Well by Doing Good provides practical advice for parishes inspired to carry out their *missio Dei* by establishing economic ventures. More than that, it offers historical, biblical, and theological perspectives on financial support of the church. This book is a must-read for parishes that are prayerfully and creatively exploring financial options to support their mission.

—**Mary Kate Wold**, chief executive officer and president, Church Pension Fund, The Episcopal Church

DOING WELL BY DOING GOOD

THE MISSIONAL BENEFITS OF CHURCH-BASED ECONOMIC ENTERPRISES

BRENDAN J. BARNICLE

FORTRESS PRESS
MINNEAPOLIS

DOING WELL BY DOING GOOD
The Missional Benefits of Church-Based Economic Enterprises

31 30 29 28 27 26 25 1 2 3 4 5 6 7 8 9

Library of Congress Control Number: 2025029345 (print)

Cover design and illustration by Brad Norr Design

Print ISBN: 979-8-8898-3643-8
eBook ISBN: 979-8-8898-3644-5

Contents

Figures

Acknowledgments

The faculty and staff at the Claremont School of Theology were essential in making this work possible. Claremont's long commitment to economic analysis, particularly the work of John Cobb, was critical for this book. In particular, Claremont professor Sheryl Kujawa-Holbrook was a source of great wisdom and guidance. As my PhD faculty advisor, she journeyed with me in developing this project. In addition, Claremont professor Andrew Schwartz provided helpful theological and ethical frameworks for the discussion of church-based economic enterprises. Claremont professor Lailatual Fitriyah was a tremendous guide when discussing decoloniality and postcoloniality. Episcopal Bishop Ian Douglas kept this work and me solidly focused on the *missio Dei.* This book also was the culmination of years of study in several other theology graduate programs. I am deeply indebted to the faculties and staffs at Church Divinity School of the Pacific, Bexley Seabury Seminary, and Santa Clara University.

Also, this work would not have been possible without the generous leaders and congregations of The Church of the Messiah in Detroit; St. Peter's Evangelical Church of Christ in Louisville, Kentucky; Grace in Action Lutheran Church in Detroit, Michigan; and St. Peter's Episcopal Church in Dartmouth, Massachusetts. They willingly shared their stories with me and took my questions. They welcomed me into their churches and into their wider communities, and they permitted me to see the *missio Dei* at work in their neighborhoods. This project would not have been possible without the outstanding editing support of Marianne Burnside and Brian Mulder, as well as Laura Gifford and the team at Fortress Press.

Finally, my wife and family have patiently supported me as I have spent years huddled in our basement working on this book. Thanks to you all.

Prelude

In December 2022, I was sitting in a board of trustees meeting for the Church Pension Group, which manages the $17 billion pension fund for the clergy and lay employees of the Episcopal Church. As a side conversation, a few of us started reviewing the current financial model of most churches, which is based on individual contributions. With declining church attendance, I started to wonder about the possibility of alternative financial models for churches. Churches could rely more heavily on endowments or rental income, but I started to wonder about churches that started businesses. For a long time, churches have rented out space and collected passive income. But what if churches operated businesses and generated active income? As I started to investigate churches that had started businesses, I was amazed to hear some wonderful stories of congregational resurrection. Churches that operated businesses, either for-profit or nonprofit, were experiencing missional renewal and congregational growth, as well as financial sustainability.

I was so impressed with these congregations that I started to discern with my own congregation about potential business opportunities. My parish is relatively secure financially, so there was not a tremendous urgency about starting a business. But everyone realized that a business might be in the church's long-term interest. Through a discernment process, we determined that an adult respite care nonprofit business would be consistent with our mission and values. We have launched that business, and we have looked to other congregations for best practices. The journey toward building it has reinforced the surprising benefits of church-based economic enterprises. There is a more detailed description of our discernment process in this book's postlude.

It is my hope that this book will help other churches to discern their call to starting economic ventures. Whether they develop for-profit businesses, business cooperatives or nonprofit organizations, churches are likely to find surprising benefits from their "sacred start-ups." Like the congregations profiled in this book, they may well find that church-based businesses offer missional renewal, congregational growth, and financial sustainability. They provide churches with the resources, both personal and financial, that are necessary to continue to carry out the *missio Dei.*

Introduction

The Paramount Network TV series *Yellowstone* tells the story of the Dutton family, owners of the largest ranch in Montana, and their desperate fight to keep it. Often, the fiercest fights happen within the family. In one climactic scene, brother and sister Jamie and Beth Dutton realize that they actually agree on one thing. The biggest threat to their family ranch is their father, John Dutton, who refuses to change the financial model of the ranch. He insists on raising cattle, even when all the facts suggest that it is the wrong choice. For John Dutton, the cattle business has been the mission of the ranch for over one hundred years, and he has no intention of changing it. He stubbornly refuses to reexamine the mission when the financial model no longer works.

Like John Dutton, there are a lot of churches that are reluctant to reexamine their missional and financial models. Leaders worry that any change to their missional model will undermine the ecclesiological institution that they have been called to steward. They also worry that changing the old financial model will destroy the tradition and mission that they have been called to carry forward. Yet if they do not change their missional and financial models, then like John Dutton, they risk losing the whole ranch.

The old ways of doing church are not working. There are numerous surveys and reports noting a decline in church attendance, membership, and financial donations. Yet there are exceptions. In many cases where churches are thriving, the congregations have taken the risk to reexamine their missional and financial models. When those congregations focused on mission and finance together, they found new life. The Holy Spirit has led them into new ways that advance social justice, address economic inequality, enhance personal agency, increase church membership, and develop economic sustainability. As a result, they are embracing the *missio Dei* (mission of God) and demonstrating new ways of reconciling God, God's people, and all of God's creation.

In this book, the *missio Dei* is frequently referenced. It is a Latin term that is defined as the "mission of God" or the "sending of God." It comprises the understanding of God's mission as reconciling all of humanity to God, to one another, and to all of creation through the example and ministry of Jesus Christ. The *missio Dei* incorporates the Christian values of the gospel, seeking social justice, inclusion, and reconciliation. The *missio Dei* also describes the goal of Christian churches, as well as the object of Christian discipleship. Christian mission has historically focused on evangelism and education, but this book seeks to demonstrate how the *missio Dei* can guide economic enterprises too.

Toward that end, this book investigates four faith communities who have incubated or started economic enterprises and subsequently experienced missional renewal, congregational growth, and financial sustainability: The Church of the Messiah in Detroit; St. Peter's Evangelical Church of Christ in Louisville, Kentucky; Grace in Action Lutheran Church in Detroit; and St. Peter's Episcopal Church in Dartmouth, Massachusetts. The first two churches are largely African American congregations. The third congregation is a Latino congregation that is led by a white pastor. The fourth congregation is a white congregation in a rural community in Massachusetts.

These faith communities are profiled in chapter 2. For this project, an "economic enterprise" can be a for-profit or nonprofit venture. It can include for-profit companies, business cooperatives, and nonprofit organizations. It can be owned by the church or merely incubated at the church and owned by individuals. In all cases, the economic enterprises are ways of driving the missions of these churches. However, the churches are less focused on the operations of the enterprises and more focused on providing the tools and support so that others can start enterprises. Finally, in all cases, the economic enterprises generate positive cash flows that support the churches. In one case study, the church owns a business through a nonprofit organization that supports new business development; in two other cases, the churches offered space and expertise to help individuals start new for-profit businesses; and in the fourth case, the church founded a nonprofit that is housed on its campus. Throughout this book, these entities will be referred to as "church-based economic enterprises," even though some of the businesses no longer operate on a church's premises.

To test whether these four case studies were anomalies, research for this book included surveys of individuals and clergy who are members of churches with economic enterprises. These survey results are summarized in chapter 3. Unfortunately, no religious denomination currently tracks such enterprises, so surveys of clergy and lay individuals offered one way of access to this information. The survey results were quite startling. In one survey of 224 individuals whose churches had developed enterprises that contribute at least 15% of the church's revenue, 90% of the respondents reported an increase in mission and membership after starting the enterprise. While increased membership is easy to quantify, mission is not. The *missio Dei* is very expansive and can include all of creation. The surveys asked people how increased mission was manifested in their church. Respondents were given several options, including increased community engagement, more outreach, additional educational programs, greater member involvement, and heightened volunteerism, which are all different expressions of the *missio Dei*. In the case studies, there was also clear evidence of missional renewal, but it was more evident in the passion and activism at each church, rather than in any of the specific characteristics noted in the surveys.

In a second survey of 261 individuals whose churches had developed economic enterprises that contribute at least 15% of revenue, 79% reported an increase in mission after starting the enterprise and 77% of the respondents reported an increase in membership. Most impressive, in a survey of 65 clergy at churches with economic enterprises that contribute at least 15% of revenue, 92.5% reported an increase in mission after starting an economic enterprise and 94% reported an increase in membership.

The case studies herein also demonstrate that the church-based economic enterprises can reduce racial and economic inequality in neighborhoods of historically marginalized people, which are also bold expressions of the *missio Dei.* While it is difficult to quantify the impact of their missional work, the churches studied for this book have enhanced the overall health of their communities and particularly their economic health. By supporting individuals in developing new businesses, they increased those individuals' agency. They are also helping to unlink economic enterprises from historical forms of business creation, which preserved the economic status quo and reinforced legacy economic colonialism. These new businesses are not beholden to the source of the start-up capital for the business or a franchisor, as has been the case historically when starting a new business venture. These congregations are creatively living into Jesus's command to preach the gospel and to heal the sick. By bringing new economic life to their communities and to individuals, these churches boldly embody the resurrection by demonstrating the emergence of new life. They are also overcoming vestiges of racism and colonialism by demonstrating that there is much to learn from historically oppressed and marginalized people. They are proving that marginalized communities may be better able to offer economic alternatives to global capitalism than existing economic powers. They are helping individuals and communities to claim their economic agency. Finally, they are starting an important conversation about the role of churches in fostering economic growth, community development, and missional renewal that break from patterns of the past that do not serve the *missio Dei.*

In reviewing these case studies and surveys, eight best practices have emerged for congregations that are open to supporting economic development as a means of pursuing the *missio Dei*. In reviewing these eight best practices, I have found they are practices that also support individual discipleship. They reinforce the *missio Dei* for both congregations and individuals. I track these practices throughout the case studies, returning to them in context of practical theological considerations in chapter 4:

1. **The primary focus must be missional, not financial.**
2. **A clergy person does not need a business background to support economic enterprises.**
3. **Leaders need to be committed for the long-term.**
4. **All leaders must be willing to experiment.**
5. **Active lay leadership is essential.**
6. **Mission emerges from supporting people on the margins.**
7. **Congregations must know their local ecosystem.**
8. **Faith and mission must be at the center.**

These practices have enabled churches to support their members and their neighbors while also supporting themselves financially. However, they are a dramatic break from the recent past. Historically, churches in the United States have relied upon charitable giving to support their operations; yet, over the last twenty years, donations have declined. For example, since 2000, individual donations have accounted for only 60% of the revenue of Episcopal churches.[1] The remaining 40% of Episcopal church revenue has come from endowments, rental income, and other revenue. Yet, despite the decline in individual giving, there has not been a meaningful change in the Episcopal church's financial model, or the financial model of any other mainline Protestant denomination in the United States.

There is mounting evidence that charitable donations, including church donations, are dropping faster than previously.[2] As a result, churches are being required to reexamine their financial models.

Fortunately, when they reexamine their financial models, they also have the opportunity to reexamine their missional models. While mission and finance are typically thought of separately, they are, in fact, tightly coupled. This book investigates the current financial "crisis" in churches, and it seeks to demonstrate that this "crisis" is an opportunity for missional renewal.

In their foundational work on practical theology, professors James Poling and Donald Miller suggest that practical theology occurs when communities of faith are reaching out in mission.[3] They argue:

> Practical theology is critical and constructive reflection within a living community about human experiences and interactions, involving a correlation of the Christian story and other perspectives, leading to an interpretation of meaning and value, and resulting in everyday guidelines and skills for the formation of persons and communities.[4]

Embedded in their understanding of practical theology is the idea that the small details of life and faith matter to the embodiment of theology. The small things that we do in church, and in those relationships that we develop along the way, inform the ways that we heal and grow, whether it involves healing from the impacts of natural disaster, climate change, or the Covid-19 pandemic.

The goal of this book is to answer four questions:

1. What do church-based economic enterprises have to do with discipleship and missiology?
2. How can churches change their missional and financial models?
3. Can church-based economic enterprises have any impact on missional vitality or congregational growth?
4. What is the role of practical theology in fostering church-based economic enterprises?

CHRISTIAN CALL FOR ECONOMIC JUSTICE

Scripture scholar Walter Brueggemann argues that economics sits at the core of the Bible.[5] There are approximately five hundred references to prayer in the Bible, and over two thousand references to money and possessions.[6] Jesus frequently discussed money. In fact, he mentioned money second only to the kingdom of God. By one count, 62% of Jesus's parables refer to money and possessions.[7] Jesus's Jewish tradition was keenly focused on the theological and biblical aspects of money. Genesis and the Psalms declare that all things, including money, come from God, and Deuteronomy insists that money must be managed with an eye toward justice.[8] Jesus was familiar with Deuteronomy's prohibition on usury and the calls for Sabbath, a Year of Release, and Jubilee—traditions which sought to free people from institutionalized debt and economic inequality.[9] Many of the recurring themes in a Christian theological discussion of money are rooted in the First Testament, particularly the Decalogue and Deuteronomy. Jesus understood these themes and incorporated them into his teaching and ministry.

To demonstrate this point, Brueggemann argues that the Deuteronomy calls for a covenant between all humans and God, which includes "economic neighborliness."[10] Deuteronomy articulates an ethical use of money in response to the predatory practices that had worked their way into Israel's economy. Deuteronomy introduced the Year of Release, which cancelled all debts in their seventh year (Deut 15:1–11) and issued prohibitions on usury (Deut 23:19–20; Deut 24:10–13, 17; Deut 24:14–15; Deut 24:19–21). In addition, Deuteronomy provided a renewed focus on the needs of one's neighbor. In particular, it called for protection of the most vulnerable: widows, orphans, and immigrants.[11] Brueggemann points out that in a predatory economy, like Israel's during the writing of Deuteronomy, the economically powerful are trying to exploit the poor and weak. Therefore, Deuteronomy seeks to replace a privatized economy with an economy that includes social protections for all people.[12] The challenge of economic neighborliness resonates through the subsequent books of Scripture.

The Psalter reiterates the ethical standards outlined in Deuteronomy. Psalm 112 describes the benefits that come to the person who gives to the poor, lends freely, and operates with justice. Psalm 112 reinforces the notion that righteous behavior is supposed to create good outcomes for the individual, and more important, for the community.[13] Psalm 49 goes further when it reminds readers that it is impossible to take wealth beyond this life. Wealth cannot provide security, because security comes only from God.[14] Trusting in anything other than God runs the risk of idolatry. In Proverbs, wisdom is attributed to the person who behaves responsibly with money, and that responsibility includes providing hospitality to those in need. Proverbs 1:19 also warns the greedy: "Such is the end of all who are greedy for gain; it takes away the life of its possessors."

Jesus consistently addressed these themes in his ministry. In the gospels, he advocated for an alternative economy that included a set of social practices and relationships consistent with covenantal Judaism.[15] In this economy, wealth would be seen as a gift from God to be used for God's people and for God's creation. Wealth had an appropriate place in the *missio Dei*. Christian notions of justice strive for the inclusion of all people in God's creation and for sharing all resources. In Jesus's "alternative economy," people would avoid envy, rivalry, and individualism in favor of love, grace, and community.[16] Despite the strong suspicion of wealth in Scripture, Christianity has been conflicted about wealth, partly because the core Christian teachings are not entirely consistent.

The early church adopted two different and somewhat conflicting views of wealth. On the one hand, Jesus was deeply skeptical about money and possessions, but on the other hand, he recognized the importance of money for providing support and hospitality to those in need.[17] Biblical scholar Sondra Ely Wheeler characterizes these approaches to wealth as "peril and obligation," each of which demands different behavior.[18] Jesus's suspicion about money is evident in his response to the "rich young ruler," who he directs to sell everything and follow him (Matt 19:16–29, Mark 10:17–30, Luke 18:18–30).[19] He also commends the rich tax collector Zacchaeus for paying back those whom he had defrauded and for giving half of his possessions to the poor (Luke 19:9). The Sermon on the Mount captures these two views of wealth. Jesus begins by reinforcing the importance of almsgiving and the obligations of wealth. "Give to everyone who begs from you" (Matt 5:43). Then, he proceeds to advise his listeners to rely upon God, and not upon individual wealth: "No one can serve two masters . . . You cannot serve God and riches" (Matt 6:35). Since these admonitions are not entirely consistent, it is understandable that Christians have developed conflicting understandings of wealth.

Throughout Christian history, theologians have articulated a commitment to shared wealth, which they have based on Scripture. Chapters 2–5 of the Acts of the Apostles illustrate how the early Christians shared their money communally, and they established community standards.

> All who believed were together and had all things in common; they would sell their possessions and goods and distribute the proceeds to all, as any had need. (Acts 2:44–45)

> Now the whole group of those who believed were of one heart and soul, and no one claimed private ownership of any possessions, but everything they owned was held in common. (Acts 4:32)

In addition to the Acts of the Apostles, the Didache provides one of the earliest references to shared wealth.[20] Similarly, the Epistle of Barnabas, which scholars believe was written around 135 CE, describes sharing wealth and possessions.[21] As early as the second century, theologian Clement of Alexandria developed the first Christian theological treatise on faith and wealth. He cautioned Christians about the dangers of wealth but also stressed that wealth is not inherently corrupting.[22] He understood that wealth had a role in God's mission.

The second-century Apostolic Father Hermas, along with Clement of Rome and Ignatius of Antioch, proposed almsgiving as a means for wealthy people to share their resources with God's people.[23] By the fourth century, Basil of Caesarea openly criticized the aggressive accumulation of wealth and proposed a sufficiency test for personal spending and consumption. His sufficiency test held that individuals keep only the money and property that they needed for their basic survival. He called upon Christians to share the rest of their wealth with others.[24] Historian Peter Brown observes that while the early Christians were critical of wealth, few of them actually had any wealth. The initial Christian discourse on wealth impacted only a very small portion of the world's population, because most people, including early Christians, lived in subsistence poverty.[25]

Theologian Justo González notes that after the fourth century, economic issues received much less attention from church theologians.[26] After Constantine made Christianity the official religion of the Roman Empire, the post-Constantinian church attracted wealthier people. Subsequently, the church was far less critical of wealth. The Roman Catholic Church spoke less than the early Christians about the peril of wealth and more about the obligations of wealth.[27] As the Roman Catholic Church grew, it moved from renunciation of wealth toward an emphasis on detachment from wealth. Theologians started to develop a virtue of sufficiency, like the one first articulated by Basil.[28] Over time, however, the church became increasingly supportive of wealth. Augustine famously called wealth a mysterious "charisma." He taught that wealth should be used to extend the influence of the church.[29] However, Augustine was not necessarily as focused on how wealth could increase the broader responsibilities of the *missio Dei*. By the seventh century, the church also had developed a very strong financial position of its own. By some estimates, the Roman Catholic Church controlled as much as one-sixth of all the land in medieval Europe.[30] Not surprisingly, with its increase in power and wealth, the Roman Catholic Church was increasingly supportive of the economic status quo.

Since the sixth century, there have been theologians and religious leaders who have raised concerns about the church's ambiguous position on wealth. For example, in the sixth century, Benedict of Nursia established strict prohibitions against private ownership in his monasteries, and he stressed the importance of sharing necessities.[31] In the eleventh century, Francis of Assisi cautioned against greed, which he defined as wanting more than what one needed to survive. In the fourteenth century, Thomas Aquinas vehemently argued that greed was antithetical to God. He condemned usury and wrote about the ethical pricing of goods.[32] In the sixteenth century, Protestant reformers Rudolf Gwalther and Peter Walpot stressed the importance of caring for those in need and the priority of sharing goods in common.[33] They represented an attempt within the Reformation to return to some of the church's pre-Constantine positions on wealth and equity. In the eighteenth century, John Wesley renewed Basil's call for sharing resources and for adopting a virtue of sufficiency. He laid out strong expectations for Christians' obligation to care for the poor. Like Basil, he insisted that Christians use their money to cover only their basic necessities and to give the remainder to the poor.[34] He established standards that provided economic guidance for individuals based on his Christian theology.

In the early twentieth century, Walter Rauschenbusch introduced the Social Gospel as another reaction to excessive wealth. He argued that the Social Gospel was merely attempting to bring Christianity back to its pre-Constantinian mission by expressing a deep care for the poor and a skepticism of wealth.[35] Over the years, other voices have observed the economic injustice in humanity's midst and the ways that economic injustice contradicted the *missio Dei*. Christian Socialism, the Catholic Worker Movement, and other faith-based groups have tried to return to a notion of wealth as peril and obligation, but they have found little support in mainstream Christianity.[36] Instead, the Christian theology of wealth and money has largely been determined by those with the greatest wealth. For example, in the early twentieth century, Andrew Carnegie and John T. Rockefeller both published theologies of wealth that largely blessed their riches and the privileges of those like them. Their voices and those of their acolytes overpowered the voices of those who were skeptical of wealth and saw wealth as a challenge to God's mission. In the mid-twentieth century, Msgr. John Ryan drew on the Thomist virtue of temperance to argue for a virtue of sufficiency. He developed a social economic ethic that provided for living wages for working people. He even enumerated what expenses should be covered by the living wage.[37] His advice was imminently practical, and it demonstrated the application of practical economic theology to livable wages and individual spending.

In the late twentieth century, Latin American liberation theology again sought to offer an alternate view of wealth. Gustavo Gutiérrez and Ignacio Ellacuría focused on the link between salvation and liberation. Ellacuría more explicitly focused on praxis, arguing that a liberating praxis is necessary for social transformation.[38] For him, liberation frees humans from material oppression, political repression, and rampant individualism.[39] The poor are critical participants in a liberating praxis. Therefore, he concluded that the church must be "configured as a church of the poor."[40] His work was deeply decolonial because he tried to unlink the church from wealth and tried to offer a new view of liberation and salvation. Like Rauschenbusch and Ryan, Gutiérrez and Ellacuría offered a renewed skepticism of wealth and demonstrated how it can interfere with the *missio Dei*.[41]

As Christians consider liberation and salvation, they are compelled to action. In addition to journeying with the oppressed, Christians are called to ask, "What liberative action should I follow now?"[42] The answer to this question requires careful discernment. Christianity has the potential to advance social justice by offering economic alternatives that reflect Jesus's views on money and wealth. It is clear from Ellacuría's work and from the case studies in this book that careful discernment is a key element of liberation and mission. Understanding God's call is the first step toward missional renewal, congregational growth, social justice, and financial sustainability. Unlinking wealth from God and from the church is critical to understanding God's mission for humanity and creation.

Consistent with these past theologians, this book seeks to provide an alternative view of wealth and possessions. Ultimately, the goal of this project is to highlight the hopeful message that churches can offer to the world when they change their missional and financial models. They can start new economic enterprises, and they can help others to start new enterprises. Collectively, churches and the businesses that they incubate can demonstrate new ways of transacting commerce and economic activity. They can create enterprises that are unlinked from past economic practices and oppressive economic systems. In so doing, they can drive missional renewal, social justice, and financial sustainability. In terms of global capitalism, church-sponsored economic enterprises may seem too small to make any difference. However, as these case studies reveal, these enterprises can make a big difference to their congregations and in their local communities. They can offer a new perspective and new hope to their neighbors by offering a new economic vision. When guided by the Holy Spirit, these churches can make changes that more fully reflect the presence of the Triune God in the world today and the liberation of all God's creation, thus advancing the *missio Dei*. Unlike John Dutton, the church must not live in a nostalgia for the past. Instead, the church can lead God's people boldly into the future with new missions, new models, and new visions of becoming God's Beloved Community.

CHAPTER 1

Practical Theology of Economics

Business management, vocational direction, entrepreneurship, and personal spending have deeply theological and missiological implications, but there has been relatively little reflection on these topics in practical theology. Most of the practical theology of money and economics has developed out of the prosperity gospel and Business as Mission (BAM), which have not necessarily prioritized the liberation of all creation as the church's primary mission. Instead, they have prioritized institutional growth, which has been focused more on ecclesiology than missiology. For practical theologians James Poling and Donald Miller, practical theology explores the impact of socioeconomic, political, and psychological biases on achieving God's mission in creation.[1] Therefore, they emphasize the importance of integrating empirical sciences into any community-based understanding of Jesus Christ.[2] They encourage faith leaders to integrate advances in science into their ministries, which they argue will ultimately enhance the mission of Christian communities.[3] While practical theology has made great strides toward integrating much of modern science and social science into theological discussions, there is still relatively little practical theology of economics.

A practical theology of economics seeks to illuminate more than just the prosperity gospel and BAM. Practical theologian Richard Osmer offers three essential elements for interpreting practical theology.[4] All three elements offer ways of understanding the practical theology of economics, as well as a theological and missiological approach to church-based economic enterprises. First, Osmer suggests that practical theology should provide a way of utilizing theological concepts to interpret daily situations and diverse contexts. Second, practical theology should aid in developing ethical guidelines, which could be applied to economic decision-making. Third, practical theology should focus on the Christian traditions that have provided guidance for a "Christian life." Osmer's three guidelines refine a liberative practical theology of economics.

To incorporate both practical theology's interdisciplinary nature, as suggested by Poling and Harris, and its interpretive value, as suggested by Osmer, there are four themes that must be addressed in any critical discussion of church-based economic enterprises.

First, there is a growing movement based on the prosperity gospel, and to a lesser extent, Business as Mission. In critiquing this theme, it is important to examine the ways in which these theologies reinforce colonialism and the status quo. They are not focused on the liberation of all of God's creation. Therefore, they can be a distraction that draws people away from gospel values and the *missio Dei*.

Second, there is growing research evaluating alternative economic models for churches and the impact of those models on mission, social justice, and economic sustainability. Most of this research has focused on church planting. Many church plants have included business operations, like coffee shops and brew pubs, to fund a new ministry. Studies of church plants reveal some helpful background information. However, most of this research has focused on ministry development and community organization, rather than business development, community economic development, and social justice. There are also some helpful insights from the burgeoning field of "redemptive entrepreneurship." Redemptive entrepreneurship seeks to integrate research in social entrepreneurship with faith settings.[5] It builds on many of the fundamental elements of asset-based community development (ABCD).[6] When faithfully implemented, redemptive entrepreneurship can demonstrate the *missio Dei* in the current global economic context.

Third, a deep consideration of decoloniality and postcoloniality provides some valuable guidance for church-based economic enterprises, and it can minimize the possibility of repeating past sins. Decoloniality is a particularly important consideration for Christian churches because of Christianity's persistent role in establishing colonialism around the world.[7] While capitalism was built on imperialism and colonialism, church-based economic enterprises might be able to deconstruct some of capitalism's colonial past.[8] The economic enterprises described in the case studies in this book offer a constructive resistance to coloniality while advancing social justice and liberation for all of God's creation, the *missio Dei*.

Fourth, when starting an economic enterprise, there are several practical considerations. First, churches will need to be deliberate in their discernment process. How and why these churches form economic enterprises will be critical to the impacts of those enterprises. With careful discernment, it is possible to offer a new form of economic enterprise that is consistent with God's mission for creation. More practically, churches need to be careful to protect their nonprofit status. If they develop a for-profit business, they will need to pay the necessary taxes. They will also need to observe all wage and hours laws and consider the impact of any new economic enterprise on their property and grounds. Fortunately, there is abundant legal, accounting, and tax advice that is available for church-based economic enterprises. As soon as these economic enterprises are successful, they are likely to face enhanced competition from more powerful economic interests that will feel threatened by them. Despite the challenges in starting a new venture, successful economic enterprises can arise from marginalized communities, and ultimately, demonstrate God's creative power and humanity's missional role. These new enterprises can be a source of inspiration and hope for an entire community, as they have been in the case studies outlined below.

PROSPERITY GOSPEL AND BUSINESS AS MISSION

Despite the calls by various Christian scholars and theologians to reform the current economic system, the most prominent contemporary Christian voices have largely reinforced it. Both the prosperity gospel and the BAM initiatives endorse profit and wealth as evidence of God's favor. They see the Mission of God as Business as Mission.

Church historian Kate Bowler chronicles the history of the prosperity gospel. She traces its roots to the New Thought movement of the late nineteenth century. New Thought combined metaphysics and Protestantism in a unique way that reflected the popularity of "mind-power" in the Victorian era.[9] It introduced a Christian anthropology that did not rely entirely on God for salvation but drew upon human potential as well.[10] It also envisioned the world as consisting of thought more than concrete substances.[11] As a result, New Thought made the bold claim that humanity actually shared in divine power because of the power of human thought.[12] In many ways, New Thought laid the groundwork for later developments that emphasized the power of positive thinking. Originally, the New Thought movement and the prosperity gospel were focused on physical health. Over time, the prosperity gospel evolved to also embrace material wealth as a sign of God's blessing.

Kate Bowler credits Essek William Kenyon as the first proponent of the prosperity gospel. Kenyon maintained that living by Christian principles would give individuals access to all of God's blessings, and he taught Christians how to capitalize on those blessings.[13] Kenyon interpreted Jesus's statement "If you ask anything in my name, I will do it" (John 14:14) as a legal and binding divine obligation. In fact, he changed the verb "ask" in John 14:14 to "demand."[14] Kenyon's work was aided by contributions from F. F. Bosworth, a leading Pentecostal of the era, and by several prominent African American leaders in northern cities. African American leaders, like Prophet James Jones, Father Divine, Father George Hurley, and the Reverend Ike, preached the prosperity gospel because it offered a hopeful theology with a vision for a life with less suffering than characterized much of the African American experience in Northern cities.[15] As a result, key themes of the prosperity gospel continue in African American churches today.

The prosperity gospel was also reinforced by the leading industrialists of the nineteenth century. Andrew Carnegie famously published his *Gospel of Wealth*, and John D. Rockefeller wrote and distributed similar materials. The prosperity gospel withstood a backlash against wealth that resulted from the extreme wealth inequality of the late nineteenth century. As mentioned previously, Walter Rauschenbusch and the Social Gospel emerged in reaction to the poverty and inequality of the late nineteenth and early twentieth centuries. However, the Social Gospel has largely faded away, whereas the prosperity gospel has strengthened throughout the twentieth century. In her book *The Gospel of Church*, Indiana University historian Janine Giordano Drake describes the ways that mainline Protestants in the United States actively worked to discredit Christian Socialism and the Social Gospel, as well as the emerging union movement.[16] Ultimately, Drake concludes that the early twentieth-century Federal Council of Churches succeeded in assuring that American Christianity never challenged the political and economic status quo. Moreover, the Federal Council never even envisioned such a critique as within its role.[17] As a result, feminist theologian Carter Heyward concludes that contemporary American Christians not only assume that capitalism is the American way of doing business, but they also assume that capitalism is the will of God.[18]

By the mid-twentieth century, the prosperity gospel had moved well beyond its initial focus on health. It was no longer considered logical that one could be truly healthy if one was not also wealthy.[19] In fact, under the prosperity gospel, wealth became a God-given right of faithful Christians. Prosperity gospel leader Kenneth Copeland concluded that "the gospel to the poor is that Jesus has come and they don't have to be poor anymore."[20] Ministers of the prosperity gospel boldly proclaimed that a faithful Christian would see their faith produce visible financial results.[21] Several leaders of the movement claimed that Jesus was also wealthy himself. For example, Pastor

Creflo Dollar points to the gifts from the Magi as evidence that Jesus was rich from birth. Gold, frankincense, and myrrh were expensive gifts meant for a king, and they demonstrate Jesus's early wealth.[22] Over time, this belief in Jesus's power to materially enrich Christians evolved into a money-back guarantee. Prosperity gospel evangelists developed formulas for financial returns based on one's tithing to their churches. The "hundredfold blessing" became the most common calculus. Churchgoers were told that God would return to the tither one hundred times their tithe.[23] Therefore, a gift of $100 to the church would pay dividends of $10,000 for the faithful givers.

In the 1990s, prosperity preachers added an entrepreneurial focus to the prosperity gospel.[24] Churches started to offer debt counseling, tax write-off advice, job banks, and small business loans.[25] They emphasized upward mobility rather than sudden financial windfalls. In all of these activities, the focus remained on individual financial success as evidence of Christian discipleship. They continued to encourage profits, capital accumulation, and personal wealth. Creflo Dollar argued that "God is the one giving us the power to get wealthy."[26]

The prosperity gospel is a fundamental component of the largest Christian congregations in the United States. Nearly half of the churches with over ten thousand members preach it.[27] Unfortunately, their fixation on wealth frequently ignores the essential painful elements of Jesus's life and ministry. For instance, in prosperity gospel churches, there is a limited recognition of Good Friday.[28] The pain of the crucifixion does not fit within the narrative of victory and success that marks the prosperity gospel. As a result, the prosperity gospel distorts Jesus's life and the depth of his theology when it is inconvenient or inconsistent with the prosperity message. Jesus identified with the poor and the outcast, and he experienced rejection and suffering himself. Those crucial elements of Jesus's life are incongruent with the prosperity gospel narrative. Therefore, they are often overlooked or ignored.

In addition, some former prosperity gospel congregants complain of spiritual competitiveness.[29] The prosperity gospel's focus on worldly success and upward mobility leaves little room for illness, failure, or doubt. People who have left prosperity gospel congregations share that they felt compelled to highlight the positive things in their life and never admit to anything negative. When those churches have engaged in outreach, they have offered individual solutions, rather than structural responses to societal challenges, like racial and economic injustice.[30] In response to racism, they encourage individuals to develop diverse multicultural friendships or attend multicultural worship services, rather than engaging in political actions seeking to dismantle white supremacy.[31] In response to poverty, they offer financial assistance, job placement and training, as well as financial counseling. While these programs are helpful, they do not address the fundamental challenges that the existing economic system imposes on people without resources.

The prosperity gospel has several weaknesses. First, like the current economic system, it focuses almost exclusively on the individual, and it fails to honor the communalism of the body of Christ theology, the social Trinity, and the *missio Dei*. Body of Christ theology refers to the apostle Paul's analogy of God's creation to a human body. Each of God's creations acts as a different part of the body. All the parts are equally important even though they serve different functions, just like a human body. Second, it fails to acknowledge that God's creation extends beyond humans to all of God's creatures and to the natural world. The prosperity gospel has little regard for the impact of individual economic decisions on others or on the planet. Even people who fail to achieve its goals still do environmental and communal harm, even if unintentional, in their pursuit of individual prosperity.[32] Third, the prosperity gospel focuses narrowly on the positive elements of human experience, and suggests that suffering, failure, and tragedy are not of God's province. They argue that if one believes in divine omnipotence, then everything in this world comes from God, including triumph and tragedy, and a believer can choose to focus exclusively on God's triumphs. Fourth, the prosperity gospel selectively examines Jesus's life, and it distorts Scripture as a means of glamorizing wealth. As a result, the prosperity gospel can ultimately prove unsatisfying and cynical to many people who follow its dictates, but who fail to find wealth, health, and happiness. Fifth, because of the prevalence of the prosperity gospel, very few Christians think critically and ethically about the current global economic system or their individual role in it. Rather, they see wealth as their God-given right and entitlement.[33] As a result, Christians have failed to raise their collective voice to denounce the greed and violence that are propagated by the current system.[34]

On the other hand, the prosperity gospel encourages people to envision a new story for their lives. It refuses to accept people's current conditions as permanent. It inspires entrepreneurship, and in some ways, it has supported people in their economic endeavors. In this respect, it shares some of the positive elements of the case studies described in this book. However, unlike the case studies, the prosperity gospel has not demonstrated a commitment to social justice, and it does not challenge the existing economic hegemony in any meaningful way. One beautiful element of the case studies in this book is the way in which these economic enterprises have benefited the entire congregation, not just those involved in the businesses. Their successes have provided hope and agency to the entire community. They have provided a new vision of what human dignity looks like. The congregations in the case studies are not suggesting that everyone has to start an economic enterprise, but they are providing a glimpse into a new world. They are showing ways to unlink from past oppressive practices and fully live into the life to which God is calling them.

A logical extension of the prosperity gospel is the BAM initiative. In recognition that God is responsible for all of creation, including businesses, BAM advocates look to businesses as an expression of their Christian discipleship and mission. BAM is defined as "a for-profit commercial business venture that is Christian led, intentionally devoted to being used as an instrument of God's mission (the *missio Dei*) to the world, and it operates in a cross-cultural environment, either domestic or international."[35] BAM was introduced by Luis Bush in 1990, and it was initially focused on less economically developed countries in Africa and East Asia.[36] Since then, BAM has been implemented in a variety of developing economic regions.[37] Supporters thought that the introduction of businesses into these parts of the world could be an effective means of introducing Christianity. But the obvious parallels to colonialism were not evident to the early advocates of BAM. They failed to recognize that they looked so similar to colonizers of the past who sought to introduce Christianity to new parts of the world, while also extracting resources from them. Instead, they viewed BAM as rising from the "ashes of colonialism."[38] They may have viewed their activities as postcolonial, but they were really recolonizing.

BAM usually emerges as microenterprises, which are small business operations, much like the enterprises that will be profiled in the case studies in this book.[39] However, unlike the case studies, they are not focused on social justice, decoloniality, or a broader understanding of the *missio Dei*. BAM advocates reject any activities that are not directly related to the business or to their mission, which is largely defined as converting people to their form of Christianity.[40] They are exclusively focused on a coupling of business and mission as a way to faithfully follow the gospels. They overlook or undervalue other aspects of Christian faith, mission, and discipleship.

Unfortunately, when churches engage in economic enterprises, there is the opportunity for corruption and abuse. There are examples of prosperity gospel/BAM churches using their influence with their members for personal economic gains. For example, in 2017, the wireless carrier Vodacom South Africa announced a partnership with the Shembe Church to sell cellular telephone subscriptions to its 6.7 million members.[41] The partnership was formerly structured with and benefited the Shembe Family Trust, which handles the financial affairs of the church, rather than the whole congregation. The Shembe Family Trust was subsequently embroiled in a larger conflict that emerged in the church after the death of its founder, Inkosi Velani Shembe, in 2011. At the time of the deal, 2.4 million of the church's members were already Vodacom customers, and the church used its influence with its members to sign the remaining

4.3 million members as subscribers with Vodacom. The Shembe family is accused of having taken all of the profit from this partnership; it was not shared with the congregation. While this is an unfortunate story, it demonstrates the potential for abuse that arises when churches engage in economic ventures without a grounded focus on the *missio Dei*.

EVALUATION OF ECONOMIC ALTERNATIVES

In his book *Postcolonializing God*, practical theologian Emmanuel Lartey outlines a process of pastoral care that applies equally well to economic discernment. Lartey's process begins with situational analysis, then shifts to theological analysis, which is followed by a critique of theology, resulting in pastoral action, experience, and then a return to situational analysis.[42] He illustrates the flow of pastoral care as shown in figure 1.1:

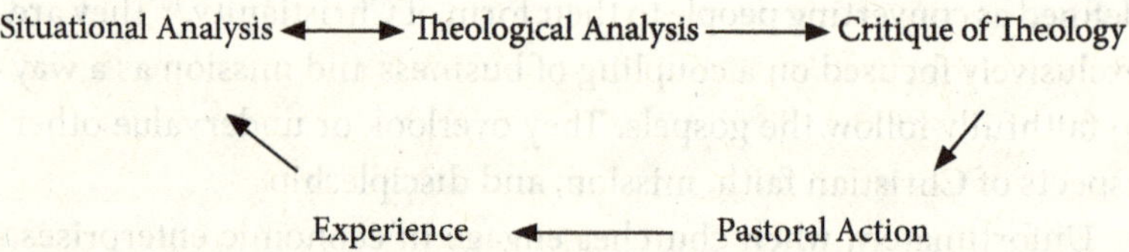

Figure 1.1. Lartey's Pastoral Care Process.
Source: Adapted from Emmanuel Y. Lartey, *Postcolonializing God: An African Practical Theology* (SMC Press, 2013).

Lartey's process outlines a healthy communal discernment process. It can also be a helpful framework for considering alternative missional and financial models for churches.

Traditionally, when churches have started businesses, they have been nonprofit organizations, which in some cases have generated some positive cash flow for the church. As a result, these businesses helped to offset the costs of traditional mission and ministry, while also demonstrating the church's broader missional impact in the world. In this way, these church-based economic enterprises do not fit within the traditional understanding of a North American business. They are not focused on executive compensation, profitability, or the accumulation of capital, like a typical North American corporation. Church-based economic enterprises also differ from B Corporations. B Corporations are corporate structures that have been approved by several states in the United States, which allow companies to prioritize a triple bottom line: employees, shareholders, and the community. B Corporations have departed from typical US corporations, which only prioritized executive management and shareholder interests. They do not have a fiduciary duty exclusively to the shareholders. The economic enterprises investigated in this book strive for sustainable cash flow, but they are not concerned with executive compensation, long-term profits, shareholder returns, or the accumulation of capital. Instead, they focus primarily on employees, the church, and the local community. Consequently, they are similar to a B Corporation because they prioritize more than just executives and shareholders. They are also different from a B Corporation because they prioritize the missional and social justice implications of their work.

Church-based economic enterprises represent a new way of conducting business that seeks to fulfill economic needs, while addressing various systemic challenges of the current economic system and thereby advancing the *missio Dei*. Specifically, these economic enterprises attempt to dismantle the detrimental effects of colonialism that have persisted because of the drive to accumulate capital. And yet, it is not clear that this cooperative approach can have a material impact on systemic economic injustice. Nevertheless, these enterprises represent an alternative to the current dominant global economic system. They are a modest, yet meaningful, activity that people and churches can engage in to resist the exploitative forces of the current economic system. These church-based economic enterprises, which are typically small, offer an alternative to global capitalism. They may, over time, develop into global markets, but that prospect seems unlikely. It is more likely that they will need to contend with global competitors. Their approaches to economic activity demonstrate that local businesses started by churches can gain an advantage over global competitors because they do not need to increase executive compensation, grow profits, or accumulate more capital. Instead, resources can be applied to employee compensation and community benefits.

More important, as demonstrated in the case studies below, they can be uplifting to a community. They demonstrate a new way of doing business that provides for personal agency for the people in the business, as well as the people in the surrounding community. The case studies showcase churches that have deployed their resources to help people use their labor and talent to develop economic enterprises. However, generally, these churches have not exercised any long-term oversight over these businesses. As churches reevaluate their missional foci, they have an opportunity to embody Paul's body of Christ theology and the *missio Dei* by fostering business development in their communities. In deploying Lartey's analysis, local congregations can manifest the body of Christ in their mission through enterprises that they help to found or incubate. In particular, congregations can build connections between individuals and community. The missional work of the four congregations examined in this book clearly empowered individuals, while also fostering a stronger sense of community. They are exemplifying how local congregations can move North American culture from "I" to "we." They also demonstrate how gospel values and the *missio Dei* can permeate twenty-first-century businesses. However, since these churches exercise no long-term control over these enterprises, they are powerless to assure that the businesses always operate in line with ethical considerations. Over time, these churches will need to explore how to provide ethical formation and guidance without patriarchal control.

As churches face financial challenges, many assume that tithing and financial contributions are the only way forward. However, tithing is a relative new practice in the Christian tradition. Throughout much of Christianity's history, the state and wealthy patrons covered the churches' major expenses. Jesus himself, along with his disciples, depended upon the support of several wealthy women.

> The twelve were with him, as well as some women who had been cured of evil spirits and infirmities: Mary, called Magdalene, from whom seven demons had gone out, and Joanna, the wife of Herod's steward Chuza, and Susanna, and many others, who provided for them out of their resources. (Luke 8:2–3)

Some early Christians were critical of leaders, like the apostle Paul, who pursued a profession alongside their religious life. Critics argued that their professions revealed an unwillingness to completely put their trust in God.[43] However, many who trusted in God were also completely dependent on wealthy patrons. Acts 16 describes the financial support that Lydia provided to the early Christian community.

> A certain woman named Lydia, a worshiper of God, was listening to us; she was from the city of Thyatira and a dealer in purple cloth. The Lord opened her heart to listen eagerly to what was said by Paul. When she and her household were baptized, she urged us, saying, "If you have judged me to be faithful to the Lord, come and stay at my home." And she prevailed upon us. (Acts 16:14–15)

Scripture also mentions other wealthy patrons who supported early Christians, including Phoebe (Rom 16:2), Jason (Acts 16), Artistobulus (Rom 16:10), Stephanas (1 Cor 1:16), Onesiphorus (2 Tim 4:19), Philemon (Phil 2), and Gaius (3 John 1).[44]

Patrons became even more prevalent in churches in the fourth century. After the conversion of Constantine, Christianity began to attract wealthier Roman citizens. In the early Middle Ages, the Roman Catholic Church became financially independent. It was acquiring and managing its own land and assets, which the bishops and their clerical staffs learned to manage effectively. In fact, it was one of the first institutions to deploy professional asset management.

As a result, by the seventh century, the church was in an exceptionally strong financial position.[45]

Roman Catholic monasteries also entered into businesses to further support themselves. In fact, for over 1,500 years, Benedictine monasteries have successfully operated a variety of businesses. The Rule of St. Benedict instructs monasteries to be self-sufficient and self-supporting.[46] The Benedictines have historically operated commodity businesses, selling eggs, produce, timber, beer, wine, and other basic products. Yet, contrary to conventional economic thinking, they have retained pricing power because of their branding. Their branding has benefited from the authenticity of their ministry. They also have maintained profitability because of their cost structure. All members of the Benedictine community provide the labor for their businesses. The Rule of St. Benedict requires all monks work in some capacity. Therefore, they can control their employee costs. There are numerous examples of the successful Benedictine business model, but one of the most remarkable is St. Sixtus Abbey in Belgium. According to *The Wall Street Journal*, St. Sixtus makes one of the most sought-after beers in the world.[47] Without any marketing and without even labeling the bottles, the monks sell sixty thousand cases of their beer every year.[48] Similarly, the Trappist monks in Scourmont, Belgium sell $50 million of beer every year.[49] The Trappist monks in Spencer, Massachusetts, sell over 1.2 million jars of their preserves through retail stores across the United States.[50]

At the same time that monasteries were collecting assets and developing businesses, parish churches expanded across Western Europe. Those churches imposed a tithe on their parishioners and collected one-tenth of the agricultural produce of the local farmers.[51] The parish tithing system eventually developed into a state funding system, where the state collected the tithe and distributed it to churches. While state funding of religion is prohibited in the United States, it remains common around much of the world today. According to a recent Pew Research survey, 22% of the world's nations have an official state religion and 20% have a favored faith tradition.[52] Because state funding was not an option in the United

States, churches experimented with pew taxes, subscriptions, and other fundraisers.

In the 1840s, several prominent Christian leaders preached and wrote about the importance of individual stewardship.[53] Slowly, churches adopted more explicit tithing models. In 1877, St. Stephen's Episcopal Church in Philadelphia implemented the first recorded tithing and pledging campaign in the United States. In 1890, Chicago businessman Thomas Kane published and distributed millions of pamphlets advocating tithing. In 1895, the Wesley Chapel in Cincinnati adopted "storehouse tithing" from Malachi 3:10–12, which required a pledge of 10% of income.[54] Subsequently, several tithing societies developed across multiple denominations in the United States. In 1906, Dr. Henry Lansdell provided scholarly support for the practice in his book, *The Sacred Tenth*.[55] The results were quite dramatic. A 1904 study found that tithers gave twenty-four times more money to their churches than people who contributed by other means.[56]

In the twentieth century, stewardship became a major focus of lay and religious leaders. Although stewardship declined during periods of national crisis, it remained a regular part of religious life.[57] However, currently, there is mounting evidence that the tithing model is failing. Churches are unable to convince people to make big financial commitments to their churches. At the same time, all charitable donations are also plummeting.[58]

As a result, churches must reexamine their financial models. Historically, new models have been discussed in the context of church planting. Since church plants do not have an established base of members to tithe, they have explored alternative funding. Samuel Lee has worked to establish metrics to evaluate the impact of these church plants through his research into Entrepreneurial Church Planting (ECP).[59] ECP focuses on advancing Christian mission through a combination of business and church planting. Lee begins with the assumption that mission should be the primary goal of Christian disciples. However, he notes that there is no consensus on mission for ECP, nor any gauges of ECP programs.[60] Different church plants interpret mission differently, and they gauge success differently.

Therefore, his work attempts to identify some common indicators of missional success and impact.

Lee uses case studies to develop a consistent comparison across different ECPs, in hopes of identifying the best practices.[61] His case studies build upon one another, and document the nuances of transformational ministry in varied contexts.[62] His first case study analyzes the Redeemer Community Church (RCC) and Dayspring Partners (DP) in the Bayview-Hunters Point neighborhood of San Francisco.[63] RCC is a church planted by Grace Fellowship Community Cumberland Presbyterian Church (GFCCPC) in 2002. DP is a web development firm that started in 1997.[64] Danny Fong is the pastor of RCC and a co-founder of DP. Initially, he and the pastor of GFCCPC envisioned a space-sharing arrangement with RCC and DP. Over time, they began to see how RCC and DP could engage in joint ministry. Together, they envisioned the redemptive qualities that could exist in a work environment that was also witnessing to God's work and power.[65]

In his research, Lee discovered that traditional church planting metrics were not particularly helpful at demonstrating the success of RCC/DP's holistic mission. From 2002 to 2020, RCC's average Sunday attendance increased from 60 to 120, which does not suggest staggering success.[66] However, other evidence indicates that RCC/DP is having a transformative impact in Bayview-Hunters Point. Specifically, Lee describes how individuals' lives are being transformed by RCC/DP's unique combination of faith and business.[67] He points to RCC/DP's success in meeting three goals: relational connectedness, reflected love, and recognition of blessings.[68] Lee defines "relational connectedness" as a sense of belonging to the group.[69] Lee identifies "reflected love" as when those who are new to the church or business start to feel sufficiently included in the community that they reflect love back to the organization.[70] Reflected love is demonstrated in increased neighborliness. This includes greater accountability and responsibility, contributions to community improvements, vocational assistance, mutual and reciprocal financial support, and integrity in business transactions. Reflected love is also shown by a commitment to peace, harmony, and justice in the neighborhood.[71] Finally, Lee defines recognition of blessings as "the return that comes from the generation and stewardship of God-given resources."[72] Lee includes the following activities as examples of blessings: relationship-based investing, job placements, increased college attendance, and genuine reconciliation.[73] These three factors (connectedness, reflected love, and recognition of blessings) are apparent in all three of Lee's case studies, and they are evident in the case studies included in this book as well. Lee also examines the Blue Jean Church (BJC) and Arsenal Place Accelerator (APA) in Selma, Alabama, which share several of the characteristics noted in the case studies for this book. The BJC was formed in 2007 in the basement of the First Presbyterian Church of Selma.[74] BJC has never focused on building a traditional church; instead, it has focused on ways of integrating with the community and brings its gospel values to the disenfranchised people of Selma. Ultimately BJC/APA's work succeeds because of three key elements: good neighbors (physical proximity); neighborly love (relational proximity); and neighborly collaboration (kingdom proximity).[75] Lee defines a good neighbor as someone who demonstrates their faith in their relationships with their neighbors.[76] Neighborly love is the way that BJC/APA provides economic opportunities to people in its community. More important, BJC/APA make their neighbors aware of their economic possibilities.[77] They instill them with a sense of economic agency, and they offer them a glimpse of a new "moral imagination," which includes all people in God's abundance. Finally, neighborly collaboration is defined as the ways in which BJC/APA make it possible to facilitate flourishing through collaboration, and how they demonstrate that *missio Dei* makes it possible to serve all of God's people.[78] While these terms were not used in the case studies in this book, those values were every bit as apparent in their practices.

Finally, Lee identifies three indicators of missional effectiveness, communion formation, community building, and *oikonomia*, in his description of the Meridzo Ministries (MM) in Lynch, Kentucky. Lee defines *oikonomia* as "God's household rule."[79] Lee also views MM as a study in "spiritual renewal, relational development, and social impact."[80] These three factors are also evident in the case studies described in this book. MM began by creating connections between the residents of Lynch, which fostered community formation. These local connections occurred at MM's businesses and at its church.[81] MM's businesses also enabled individuals to become economically self-sufficient.[82] Finally, as residents developed stronger ties and as the community grew, Lynch's identity started to change. The community began to see itself as a place that was loved and that could love. The citizens began to feel a filial responsibility for one another. In this way, Lynch was embracing *oikonomia*. The members of the town began to care for each other and operated more like one family. They became more like the body of Christ and more fully understood the *missio Dei*.

In reviewing all three case studies, Lee highlights three primary findings: relationality, growth and development that was not outcome specific, and holistic transformation.[83] As in the case studies below, the financial implications of the missions are not the primary consideration. Lee does not explicitly explore how mission and finance can drive each other. Nevertheless, the case studies demonstrate how a missional focus can also result in financial sustainability. Missional models can drive financial models and vice versa. Lee's case studies, as well those in this book, demonstrate how faith organizations can help people take control of their finances, their communities, and their faith. Moreover, the benefits are not just limited to the church leaders or the entrepreneurs; everyone in these communities benefits from these ministries and these economic enterprises. They have found a new sense of dignity and envisioned new possibilities. They have more fully seen themselves in the image and likeness of God. The communities in Lee's case studies and those described in this book have largely been overlooked by the dominant forces in the global economic systems, but these churches and ministries change individual and communal life, empowering communities in dynamic new ways. Consequently, this work reduces economic inequality, and it is effective in decolonizing existing economic systems and addressing the colonialism that is still pervasive in global capitalism.

In addition to church planting, there is a burgeoning financial model, redemptive entrepreneurship.[84] This new model seeks to align missional and financial goals of Christian organizations. The term "redemptive entrepreneurship" was first used at the 2019 UnFamous Conference in Seattle.[85] It is also used by Praxis Lab, which is an incubator for faith-based social entrepreneurs.[86] Presbyterian minister and nonprofit leader Mark Elsdon argues that redemptive entrepreneurship enables communities to reimage their mission and their finances for transformation and innovation.[87] Through his research, Elsdon offers numerous examples of redemptive entrepreneurship. In addition, he recommends five necessary elements for this model to be successful.

First, Elsdon encourages churches to focus on their core mission.[88] If they focus on mission, finances can follow. Too frequently, congregations fear that focusing on financial needs will distract from their mission. However, financial challenges oftentimes help churches to prioritize and to refine mission.[89] Second, to remain focused on mission, Elsdon recommends carefully measuring the impact of the mission's outcomes.[90] He is not recommending simply keeping track of the number of people served. Rather, congregations should be looking critically at the impact of the mission on the people served. In the case studies below, congregations focused on the people they were serving, and the congregational and financial benefits followed. Third, Elsdon recommends focusing on the details of a new economic enterprise. In the case studies below, business plans were part of every initial venture. They varied in size, scope, and complexity, but they were initial attempts to bring a discipled focus to creating new economic enterprises. At times, congregations worry that a new economic enterprise will distract from the ministries of the church. But if the economic enterprise is consistent with the mission and ministries of the church, then it will enhance the congregation. However, to be effective, the church must carefully attend to the business model. Fourth, Elsdon recommends aligning mission and money, which is also very clear in the case studies below.[91] Specifically, any project that has a negative impact on mission should be automatically eliminated, even if it generates money for the congregation. Finally, congregations must embrace risk and failure.[92] Secular business literature is increasingly highlighting the value of failure. Unfortunately, churches have been remarkably risk-averse, despite the clear risks embodied in Jesus's life and ministry.

Another helpful resource for churches exploring alternative economic enterprises is the groundbreaking work of community organizing pioneers John McKnight and John Kretzmann, who developed the concept of asset-based community development (ABCD). While ABCD was developed in a secular setting, it has broad implications for churches, particularly those churches that might start or incubate church-based economic enterprises. ABCD strives to identify the assets and capacities that exist within a community, and it subsequently leverages those assets and capacities to engender new community opportunities.[93] In all three of the case studies in Samuel Lee's work, the congregations and the church leaders developed a keen understanding of the assets in their communities. When McKnight and Kretzmann first proposed ABCD, they were offering an alternative to traditional economic development, which had been driven by the needs and deficiencies in a community, rather than its assets. ABCD has been successful because it engages the entire community, encouraging the community to invest its resources in community projects.[94] ABCD is deeply empowering because it relies upon internal assets rather than waiting upon outsiders for assistance.[95]

ABCD begins by inventorying the contributions from individuals, associations, and institutions in a community.[96] It recognizes the outstanding work that is already occurring in a community; then it builds on that work.[97] Rather than focusing on the deficiencies in the community, ABCD acknowledges existing capacities in a community.[98] ABCD is a highly relational model, fostering relationships between local residents, local associations, and local institutions.[99]

To determine the individual assets in a community, ABCD gathers basic information about the talents and skills of individuals in the community. In their work, McKnight and Kretzmann offer extensive lists of skills and talents. They encourage communities to circulate these lists and collect data. Then, organizations use the data to assess how they might best work with people in the community. Practically, ABCD uses mapping to draw connections between individuals, associations, and institutions. By mapping these relationships, the community starts to see how the assets in its community can be utilized to support the community. For example, McKnight and Kretzmann highlight all of the ways that a welfare recipient is connected to many different people, associations, and institutions within the community. Therefore, rather than viewing welfare recipients as liabilities, McKnight and Kretzmann demonstrate how they are connectors.

In addition to valuing individuals, ABCD recognizes the underappreciated value of community associations.[100] Associations, like book groups, historical societies, neighborhood associations, and crime watches, gather people together in new and unexpected ways. They are not as formalized as institutions, so they are not as constrained, and they can be more responsive to the changing needs of a community. As with individuals, McKnight and Kretzmann begin by inventorying the associations in a neighborhood. They also recognize that lower-income neighborhoods typically have particularly strong and unique associations.[101] After identifying the associations and their resources, ABCD maps the connections between these associations, just like the individual mapping exercises described above.

In the same way that associations offer a powerful means of connection, ABCD also stresses the importance of local institutions for community development. McKnight and Kretzmann specifically identify the important assets that religious institutions could offer to communities. Churches have personnel, meeting spaces, facilities, office equipment, local expertise, and economic power that could be offered to support additional community development.[102] Churches can also demonstrate healthy employment practices, offer educational resources, provide financial assistance, and support young people in the community.[103] Other institutions include parks, hospitals, schools, and public institutions.

ABCD fundamentally recognizes the value of every individual, every association, and every institution. In that way, it is deeply incarnational, and it is consistent with *Misso Dei*. It recognizes the divine that exists in everyone, and it seeks to draw each individual's gifts and assets together into one community, which is also consistent with body of Christ theology.

DECOLONIALITY

Successful ABCD work has occurred in historically marginalized communities with few economic resources. Similarly, Elsdon notes that most of the redemptive entrepreneurship has occurred in Black, Indigenous, People of Color (BIPOC) communities. Both ABCD's work and redemptive entrepreneurship can be deeply decolonial. They work to dismantle the historical colonial economic systems that rely upon the exploitation of people and resources. They enable formerly exploited people to gain economic power, and they extend those benefits to the entire community. As a result, they demonstrate economic success that is delinked from historical colonial economic practices. These approaches are considered more decolonial than postcolonial because they are not simply adapting to the postcolonial realities but offering entirely new options. They are unlinked from the past and prompt the "moral imagination" to envision a world in which all people are viewed as the image and likeness of God.

A decolonial focus is particularly important before churches embark on economic enterprises. Christian churches have been huge economic beneficiaries of colonialism. Christian religious orders and missionary organizations funded part of their operations off of exploitative colonial enterprises. Across the world, Christianity was a co-conspirator with governments in establishing colonial systems that oppressed millions of people. Decolonial leader Frantz Fanon has argued convincingly that Christianity is deeply complicit with colonization, because it created divisions that enabled the colonizers to more easily dominate and control the local peoples.[104] In addition, Christianity developed an epistemology that "institutionalized the inferiority" of the indigenous people of the Western Hemisphere, which became a basis for "genocidal violence" and the "exploitation of labor."[105] As a result, European governments easily justified a system of exploitative plantations across the globe that oppressed Indigenous peoples and enslaved Africans.[106] In fact, Christian religious orders and missionary organizations themselves owned colonial plantations. In the sixteenth century, Spanish Jesuits in South America owned agricultural estates, and they exploited Indigenous labor to produce wine, sugar, and livestock. In the seventeenth century, French Jesuit priests in the Caribbean owned sugar plantations, and they enslaved people to farm its plantations.[107] Even the prestigious Jesuit institution, Georgetown University in Washington, DC, owned enslaved people and relied upon African slaves to operate the Jesuits' plantation in Maryland during the eighteenth and nineteenth centuries.[108] However, the Jesuits were not the only religious organization to exploit colonialism for their personal gain. In 1710, the Church of England's burgeoning Society for the Propagation of the Gospel in Foreign Parts (SPG) was gifted two sugar plantations and three hundred slaves in Barbados, which it continued to operate well into the nineteenth century.[109] There are countless other examples across Africa, Asia, and Australia. Therefore, churches must be mindful of Christianity's colonial past so as not to repeat any form of it with their new economic ventures.

While decolonial thought cannot right the past wrongs of a colonial economic system, it can help to dismantle it. One of the great benefits of decolonial thought is a willingness to accept that people and institutions may not always know exactly what they are doing. In developing new businesses, churches may not always know precisely what they are doing. They may not be completely competent. Theologian Christine Hong argues that notions of competence and "mastery" have been used to disempower historically marginalized people and reinforce legacy colonial power. The "power of perfection narrative" is highly effective at inhibiting change and preserving the status quo.[110] While Hong writes in a context of religious education, the colonial forces that she critiques are equally inhibiting in economic enterprises. New economic enterprises are typically viewed as new competition, even if the economic enterprise is operating in an entirely different market. Economics is still largely viewed as a zero-sum game. If a church starts a candle company, then all the other candle companies will view it as competition. Moreover, other consumer products companies will view it as competition because the new candle company makes it marginally more likely that an individual will use their limited discretionary income to buy the church's candle rather than some other consumer product.

Legacy colonial economic systems reinforce a theology of scarcity and suggest that only one new economic group can succeed at a time. As a result, colonial systems aim to create competition and animosity between diverse people seeking common liberation.[111] A theology of scarcity enables the oppressor to determine when liberation will occur for the oppressed. On the other hand, a theology of abundance suggests that, in God's creation, there is more than enough of everything for all of God's creatures. In God's abundant creation, those who have been dehumanized by an oppressor are not required to prove to their oppressor that they have a right to flourish and thrive.[112] A robust economic enterprise will make the business operator's right to exist manifestly clear to those who would oppress them. Nothing gets someone's attention like eating into their profit margins. Therefore, while church-based economic enterprises do not automatically debunk a theology of scarcity, those enterprises demonstrate that God's creation is sufficient for all of God's people, including those that the colonial system treated as outsiders. As a result, it not only offers agency to the people who start the economic venture, but to the entire community. The whole community benefits from the entrepreneur's vision and imagination. After seeing a peer chart a new path, they are more likely to envision new possibilities for themselves.

To succeed in developing new economic enterprises, churches need to boldly embrace experimentation. Hong argues that the "anticolonial antidote to the cooption of liberation is to let loose a wild imagination."[113] Again, while Hong's work focuses on teaching and learning, her observations are equally applicable to business. Moreover, if new economic enterprises incorporate the cultural, ethnic, racial, or religious differences of their operators, then those economic enterprises normalize difference in a business context, which aids in dismantling colonial economic and intellectual domination.

Another antidote to colonialism is retelling stories.[114] Hong observes that coloniality always seeks to control the narrative.[115] Telling the stories of economic enterprises that are developed by historically oppressed and marginalized people offers a new story. In these stories, the historically dominant economic players do not maintain all the control. The stories are not just limited to the entrepreneurs and the church leaders, but there can be equally powerful stories from customers, partners, and community members. Ultimately, historically oppressed and marginalized people are not just cogs in the dominant economic system. They can own the means of production, and they can use those means to transform and transcend historical colonial economic practices. They can also move beyond the binary of worker and owner, thereby offering an example of an owner of an economic enterprise who works for the entire community, and all of God's creation. They can be a business that embraces the *missio Dei*. Therefore, the stories that are shared in this research have a role to play in confronting and dismantling colonialism. They are meant to inspire other churches. Those churches can reevaluate their missional model, and with it, their financial model. Ultimately, churches can also develop economic enterprises that reduce coloniality and advance social justice for all of God's people.

Lartey argues that postcolonializing activities are designed to enable individuals to transcend the limitations set upon them by past colonial histories and the oppressive economic and social orders that have emerged from those histories.[116] While postcolonial typically describes activities that occur within a colonial context, Lartey describes seven characteristics of postcolonializing activities that can help to transcend historical colonialism and delink colonialism from new economic ventures. These characteristics are evident to varying degrees in the case studies included in this book. First, "postcolonializing activities are counter-hegemonic, insurgent, even subversive in nature and character."[117] The aspects of counter-hegemonic behavior in Lee's case studies and in the case studies in this book involve leaders willing to try starting new economic enterprises, even when conventional thinking would have suggested that they could only ever be employees. In addition, in the case studies below, it is clear that whole communities started to think differently about economics after seeing new businesses developed in their churches by their neighbors. Second, Lartey argues that postcolonializing activities must be strategic and intentionally transformative.[118] Again, Lee's case studies and those in this book have relied heavily on strategic decision-making. After strategically evaluating their assets and those in the community, these leaders designed economic enterprises that would respond to local needs and serve local people. Third, postcolonializing activities are multidimensional and rely upon hybrids of traditional economic and organizational practices.[119] As a result, these economic enterprises may not look like traditional businesses and may appear messy or chaotic to an outsider.[120] These characteristics may not be abundantly clear in Lee's case studies, but they certainly are clear in the cases featured in this book. These economic enterprises draw on an interdisciplinary approach to business formation, and they rely upon multiple unconventional approaches to new business formation, including relying upon churches as business incubators. Fourth, postcolonializing activities analyze, critique, and seek to transform historical economic practices.[121] Critical analysis is particularly important for economic enterprises because they can easily fall victim to chasing profits at the expense of other values and priorities. If these economic enterprises remain cognizant of the economic history in their communities, they can lead their enterprises in ways that overcome their colonial past. Fifth, postcolonializing activities are highly dynamic.[122] There is constant change in any economy. As a result, the organizations engaging in new economic enterprises need time for reflection, change, and analysis. The best leaders in the case studies in this book have been able to respond to the changing needs of their communities, congregations, and local businesses. By responding to those changes, they have also provided members of the community (even those who are not starting businesses) with enhanced personal agency. Sixth, postcolonializers seek as many voices as possible, particularly those voices that have not historically been included in economic conversations, in the development of their new enterprises.[123] Postcolonial leadership finds a way of collaboratively moving forward with a broad diversity of voices, which may not always agree on important topics. Seventh, postcolonializing activities are creative.[124] These case studies demonstrate immense creativity. They demonstrate how creative thinking can be incorporated into business development to address injustice and inequity. More important, Lartey describes the way in which this process relies upon "mimicry" of colonial activities to subvert and overthrow colonialism, but it can only fully prevail if it is aided by improvisation and creativity.[125]

Lartey examines these seven characteristics of postcolonializing activities in the context of African American churches.[126] He investigates the ways in which African American congregations have responded to changing surroundings and conditions. Their adaptability has been a key element of their resiliency and their faith. Similar adaptability is clear in Lee's work and in the case studies in this book. Collectively, all of the case studies demonstrate the postcolonializing potential in church-based economic enterprises. These churches are doing more than creating new financial models. They are creating new missional models that are making the postcolonializing power and character of God more fully evident in the world. They are also helping people in their communities to recognize their inherent power. While the colonial system denied their power, these churches are affirming it, and not just for aspiring entrepreneurs, but for the whole community. As a result, they are reconciling all people to God, each other, and to all of creation. They are living into the *missio Dei*.

PRACTICAL CONSIDERATIONS

Owning or operating an economic enterprise requires accountability of the people who own or operate the enterprise to the people that they serve. Hong notes that in dismantling colonialism, it is essential that all parties adhere to accountability. She examines accountability as a long-term commitment to the communities surrounding an enterprise, and to the people who have nurtured those who lead these enterprises.[127] Again, while Hong does not make this point in an economic context, it is still highly applicable to economic enterprises. Ultimately, Hong concludes that decolonial work aims to restore hope and flourishing.[128] The case studies in this book demonstrate owner accountability and offer communal hope and missional renewal. These communities and their enterprises have clearly brought hope and flourishing to their owners and operators, the surrounding communities, and the sponsoring congregations. However, the churches did not demand significant accountability. They provided ethical formation and guidelines, but they did not have any way of imposing accountability on the businesses that emerged in their midst. Going forward, churches will need to discern how to balance the need for accountability with the need to honor the independence of these economic enterprises.

Missiologist Dwight Zscheile argues that the church leaders need to be lifelong learners.[129] In his book *The Agile Church: Spirit-Led Innovation in an Uncertain Age*, Zscheile correctly observes that learning is risky, but it is also essential for innovation.[130] He also emphasizes that learning involves change; change involves loss, all of which is reflected in Scripture.[131] Zscheile posits that failure is at the core of the biblical narratives of Jesus's life.[132] Jesus took risks, and as Zscheile notes, Jesus failed hard, in a worldly sense. Jesus's disciples were shocked by the worldly failure of the crucifixion.[133] Nevertheless, Jesus provides a kind of risk profile for Christians, and particularly for Christian churches. Following Jesus's example, churches should be willing to take risks, including starting economic enterprises, to advance their mission. Moreover, churches and their leaders need a deep-seated commitment to lifelong learning, experimentation, and improvisation, which are also essential elements for any new start-up venture. In the case studies documented in this book, the clergy leaders knew very little about starting these economic enterprises. Yet, they took a chance and tried, and ultimately, they renewed their churches and their communities in the process.

Any congregation engaging in for-profit or cashflow positive businesses must be aware of the potential risks of operating in the current economic system. People can make poor decisions in their efforts to drive profits. Catholic theologian Elizabeth Liebert observes that every venture is called to serve God's creation and the *missio Dei*, including for-profit businesses. However, many economic enterprises fall short of God's call and oppress others to operate their ventures.[134] All economic enterprises can and must work nonviolently to ensure that their operations heed God's divine call, rather than individual desires.[135] Therefore, any new economic development requires careful discernment.

Discernment

In her book *The Soul of Discernment: A Spiritual Practice for Communities and Institutions*, Liebert suggests Appreciative Inquiry (AI) as a way to move an enterprise beyond a preoccupation with its own needs to focus on its broader Christian mission.[136] Even with deliberate discernment, profits can be dangerously seductive, and organizations will need to be vigilant in remaining true to their mission. Starting an economic enterprise has many risks, particularly the risk of losing focus. Nevertheless, churches in the case studies discussed in this book prove that it is possible to start healthy businesses that maintain their missional focus. Moreover, these cases underscore the importance of taking risks to reinvigorate church mission, spur congregational growth, and advance social justice.[137]

The case studies in this book highlight the ways in which churches can help people without economic power to develop economic strength, even in a system that has sought to exploit them. These churches and their enterprises illustrate ways to start the process of dismantling unjust and colonial economic systems. Liebert correctly notes that historically marginalized individuals locate where the injustice and suffering are in a system, particularly an economic system.[138] Therefore, all of God's people are called to journey alongside the economically marginalized and oppressed for the flourishing of all of God's creation, and not just the thriving of the wealthy and powerful.[139] In discussing power dynamics, Liebert points out that power looks different for the powerful than for the powerless. For the powerful, the Christian discipleship is a call to humility and to sharing resources for the good of all God's creation.[140] However, for the powerless, the same kind of humility actually takes away power and returns the powerless to the bottoms of the global hierarchies.[141] For the powerless, Liebert argues that Christian discipleship obliges people to appreciate and responsibly exercise their power.[142] It requires them to seize their agency and to prioritize the agency of others in their community.

Liebert also identifies other values that are evident from sound discernment: unity, security, progress, inclusiveness, flexibility, and care of creation.[143] While the body of Christ theology is typically applied to churches, it can be equally applicable to nonprofit and for-profit economic enterprises. They can operate in ways that honor and include all of God's creation. In addition, unified churches are in a better position to operate or incubate a successful economic enterprise than churches that lack unity. Liebert posits that a sense of security in churches grows out of an abiding trust in the institutions of a society.[144] She contrasts her understanding of security with the way in which security has been used as a justification for militarization, spying, torture, and the repression of human rights.[145] Healthy congregations and healthy economic enterprises inspire trust, and they can build broader societal trust, which extends beyond their own congregation. Similarly, church-based economic enterprises can contribute to meaningful progress on social justice. In this understanding of progress, progress is not merely measured by absolute economic growth, as reflected in statistics like Gross Domestic

Product (GDP). Rather, progress is measured by improvements for humans, as well as the planet and future generations.[146] Increasingly, there are businesses that are looking to improve the human experience, while also protecting the natural world. Church-based economic enterprises should prioritize standards of progress that are consistent with all of God's creation.

Sociologist Zygmunt Bauman argues that the current economic system treats many people like waste and refuge.[147] They are simply fodder for economic growth and profitability. The global economic system views them as either workers or consumers, but it does not honor them as full members in the Western capitalist community.[148] Those people are forever outsiders. Yet Jesus ministered almost entirely to outsiders. He fraternized with the tax collectors and the prostitutes rather than the temple authorities and Roman rulers. He recognized the human dignity of every person. Similarly, when churches help historically oppressed and marginalized people to develop economic enterprises, they are recognizing the dignity of those individuals. This approach allows all people to be full-fledged and equal members of the global economic community. This is the embodiment of the *missio Dei*.

Church Support

One of the challenges of starting an enterprise is that the current economic system requires new ones to constantly perform and compete. Their leaders must constantly look for incremental resources, skills, and advantages.[149] As a result, within the current economic system, the process of starting a new venture can be isolating and dehumanizing. Churches can provide support by using their resources and relationships to help new economic enterprises secure the resources and skills that they need to succeed. Therefore, the operators of the new economic enterprise are not alone and isolated. Rather, they can be part of a cooperative project that builds community. In the case studies, it was clear that the entrepreneurs were getting valuable support from their churches and from each other.

When churches help people start economic enterprises in historically impoverished communities, they are also bringing economic life back to neighborhoods that have suffered years of neglect. These new businesses can help to refute Bauman's claim that American "ghettos" have become nothing more than a "waste disposal tip."[150] The new economic enterprises, built on the assets of these communities, demonstrate the intrinsic value of those communities. They also serve the community in very practical ways. They reduce the chronic unemployment and mitigate understandable resentment that has come to mark these impoverished communities. These new businesses, in particular cooperative businesses, can be instrumental in rebuilding trust in communities. In all of the case studies in this book, the economic enterprises have depended upon people working together to succeed. Their ventures build relationships within a community, which fosters mutual trust. With trust, radical change is possible in any neighborhood. In many cases, the change moves beyond economics to other important community issues, like gun violence and immigration.

Churches can provide the support that vulnerable people need to develop economic sustenance, thereby enabling individuals to fully engage their agency, but not just individual agency. As a result, these economic enterprises aid in a collective form of agency. People starting them can develop greater economic autonomy, which can also lead to greater personal autonomy in other areas of their lives. They can become less dependent on an economic system that seeks to exploit them. In her discussion of vulnerability, philosopher Judith Butler describes the importance of infrastructural and architectural support for vulnerable people. For example, some individuals with physical disabilities literally need support to stand up on their own. The same need for support applies to people who have been marginalized or impoverished by the current economic system.[151] They need economic support to start new businesses. Butler cautions that the end product of these new enterprises is not some realization of "heroic individualism," but the realization of the value of communal support.[152] Church-based economic enterprises offer a different view of the current global economic system. These ventures are disrupting the status quo in their communities. They have originated on the economic margins. They are not coming from the economic mainstream. Decoloniality argues for the value that comes from the margin, and these case studies make that decolonial value clear.

While helping to start a few economic enterprises will not entirely overcome the damage of colonialism and the exploitation of the current global economy, it is something that churches can do to overcome past injustices and to live more fully into the gospel-based values of Christianity and the *missio Dei*. This approach still risks falling into the colonial pitfalls of capitalism, but it gives voice and power to those who have historically suffered exploitation by those who employed them.[153] Moreover, this approach cannot be the only response to global economic injustice. Churches cannot fall into complacency once they have helped to found an enterprise. Otherwise, they will merely continue to sustain the status quo and oppressive systems. In addition, churches have not considered a vast matrix of issues, like ethical considerations, that come from working with economic enterprises. There is much work that churches must continue to discern upon to provide the proper formation for their members and these new ventures. Nevertheless, church-based economic enterprises offer churches a constructive response to the persistent injustice in the global economy and embody an economic response to the *missio Dei*.

Communal Leadership

When leaders share power, economic enterprises and churches can demonstrate the inclusivity that marked Jesus's ministry and the *missio Dei*. In the cases examined in this book, the leadership teams focus on communal leadership. They strive to include all voices in the decision-making process, which is a profound act of faith. As Liebert notes, "Letting everyone in requires a radical trust that God will provide for all and that our task is to open our arms and hearts to others as we have been welcomed by God."[154] When churches extend themselves and start economic enterprises, they are in a better position to demonstrate inclusiveness. They are able to offer inclusiveness that extends beyond the church sanctuary and embraces the entire community. Communal leadership also relies upon flexibility. Modern businesses need flexibility to respond to a rapidly changing world. The case studies in this book reveal that churches can start or incubate economic enterprises that have flexibility that empowers their other ministries and the *missio Dei*. It is unclear whether these churches were already flexible before they started businesses, but they are clearly flexible now.

Creating new economic enterprises involves risk and change, which can make congregations reluctant to embark upon them. Some might even argue that God is not completely supportive of business development. Jesus told a cautionary parable of the farmer who built bigger barns and then died the following night (Luke 12:16–21). However, Jesus was not counseling against economic activity; he was counseling against greed. Any church-based economic enterprise must guard against greed, as well as other sins. God's creative power in the world can also be expressed in economic development, which brings new products and services into the world. In the case studies in this book, the new businesses are frequently filling a hole in their community that has been left empty by the current economic system. New ventures can provide food and medical care in communities that lack grocery stores, clinics, and hospitals. They can create jobs in neighborhoods plagued by high unemployment. Churches can provide spiritual and ethical formation and assist in discernment as people determine how God is calling each of them to live out their faith. Moreover, when churches create their own economic enterprises, they can also demonstrate what a gospel-centered venture might look like in this world. Rather than businesses that are focused primarily on profits, churches can offer examples of economic enterprises that prioritize the *missio Dei*.

There are already numerous such examples that are striving for more than profits. There are over 750 businesses in the Economy of Communion, which is part of the Catholic Focolare Movement. These businesses are committed to prioritizing social justice over profit maximization.[155] They stress collective decision-making over individualism, and cooperative relationships rather than competitive ones.[156] They hire from historically marginalized communities and pay a living wage. In many ways, they are similar to B Corporations, which seek to balance profit with social and environmental impact, but they offer an even stronger commitment to social justice and decoloniality.

Some scholars have argued that the dominant global economic system cannot be saved, because it is fundamentally oppressive and colonial. It is dependent upon exploiting the labor and talents of individuals.[157] However, these case studies illustrate that a church can help people use their labor and talent to develop their own economic enterprises, and that the benefits from these can extend beyond the entrepreneur to the entire community. Fundamentally, rather than directing these economic enterprises, churches are aiding them and learning with them. The churches can support individual agency in economic matters, as well as in other parts of people's lives. Because the churches are not assuming a patriarchal position of dominance in these case studies, the people who start these ventures are more likely to retain control of the enterprise. They are no longer patronized or desocialized by the economic system, as has oftentimes been the historical experience of nonwhite people in the United States.[158] Instead, as business owners and operators, people can contribute to the decoding and deconstructing of the sex-gender and race codes that have been used to establish and maintain colonialism, capitalism, and unjust economic structures.[159] They can recode their gender and race as symbols of power, rather than characteristics of victims. In addition, churches can move from an ecclesiological focus on themselves to a more missional focus in serving God's people. The case studies in this book illustrate how historically marginalized individuals and groups can educate and lead the historically dominant voices in the Church, revealing a new way forward through church-based economic enterprises, offering missional renewal, congregational growth, social justice, and economic sustainability. As a result, these new participants in the economy can also start to address the vulnerability and uncertainty in their own lives, finding a new way forward for themselves and for others in their communities.[160]

Audre Lorde famously observed that "the master's tools will never dismantle the master's house."[161] The master may allow the historically disenfranchised to "temporarily beat him at his own game, but they will never" allow for genuine change.[162] These economic enterprises are using the master's tools, but they are not dismantling the master's house. Rather, they are enabling people who have never had access to tools to build their own houses. At some point, the master will start to feel threatened by these new houses. When the established economic powers experience increased competition from these new enterprises, they will try to stop them through increased competition, predatory business practices, and legal entanglements. At this point, the economic enterprises described in this book are too small to capture the master's attention. However, if they start to impact competitive market dynamics, then they will receive much more attention from the "master." At first, the dominant economic powers may belittle or discredit these enterprises, but over time, they may respond more aggressively. These enterprises and the churches that support them will need to prepare themselves for that possibility. Considering how to resist these attacks will be as important as every other part of their discernment process, and it will be critical to advancing the *missio Dei* in the midst of these challenges.

In addition, these new business owners need to be sufficiently self-aware to realize that material security will never fully eliminate their own fears and uncertainties. The persistence of human fear can easily convince someone of the need to take advantage of another person financially, to exploit them for personal gain, or to make them the "other." Adam Smith famously argued that economic freedom was "akin to freedom from the forces of 'othering.'"[163] Ironically, Smith's capitalist system came to rely upon "othering" and domination to prevail. Church-based economic enterprises cannot overcome anxiety, but they may provide some momentary relief from fear, and even the possibility of hope, for those engaged with these new ventures and for their communities.[164]

New owners and operators of economic enterprises, who were once the "other," must resist the systemic inclination to ostracize and marginalize another person or group of people. Sex-gender and racial coding systems seek to reinforce the status quo and to undermine those who would challenge it.[165] These same codes that limited the opportunities for new owners and operators in the past will seek to do the same to others. The current global economic system still seeks to exploit the labor of others. Feminist ethicist Beverly Wildung Harrison observes that many people in North America suffer from "social amnesia," where they forget everything about their past experiences of oppression.[166] They deny their own family history that does not reflect the American dream of endless upward mobility. The new owners and operators must be careful that they do not repeat the injustices that were perpetrated on them.

The current economic system is remarkably proficient at absorbing and co-opting cultural, ethnic, racial, and political differences.[167] One only has to shop at a clothing retailer to see how quickly progressive slogans and markers of identity make their way onto t-shirts and into mainstream fashion. As these new church-based economic enterprises start, there will be outside forces that will want to co-opt these businesses, particularly because they tell hopeful stories. As I have studied these churches and their economic enterprises, I recognize that I am, in a sense, co-opting their stories. I am interested in telling a story about new life in the Church, missional renewal, and a new form of economic enterprise. These are my goals, but they might not be a priority for the people operating these enterprises. I hope that these stories will encourage other churches to also foster missional economic activity in their communities. While I do not perceive that my goals are malicious in any way, others may try to exploit these stories in less generous ways. New owners and operators will also need to be on guard against co-opting other peoples' stories to advance their own stories or businesses. To the extent that these new enterprises are cooperative and collaborative business enterprises, the current competitors may view them as weak and vulnerable. They may look to prey upon them.[168]

These new economic enterprises will also need to resist the economic allure of prioritizing a "society of producers," in which all people are valued based on their individual production or consumer value.[169] Since these economic enterprises are embedded in their local communities, their owners and operators will likely maintain a greater sensitivity for the vulnerable people around them. Many of their neighbors may not be producers, because they do not have the skills or ability to produce things that the economic markets value. In addition, they may not be strong consumers because they do not have the wealth necessary to support consumerism. Nevertheless, they remain the beloved children of God who are made in the image and likeness of God. The current economic system may not recognize this divine value. Individuals who are not producers or consumers can easily be overlooked or disregarded in the race for economic progress.[170] Cooperative and collaborative approaches to the current economic system, like these case studies, must find a way to retain a commitment to vulnerable people, while encouraging economic enterprises that serve the whole community. These new local economic enterprises will need to develop global sympathies, even though their work will be primarily local. Bauman observes that too often the aim of prioritizing local problems is a way to maintain the status quo and protect those in power, while ignoring the global consequences of local economic activity.[171] These owners and operators will need to strive to reverse that trend. While their economic enterprises may be small and local, they need to understand their disruptive and transformative potential.

Once these new church-based economic enterprises have been established, the church exercises no long-term oversight of the operations. A church can help to launch a for-profit or nonprofit enterprise, but it cannot be guaranteed that the enterprise will not make poor choices. These enterprises might ultimately seek to exploit others. Some churches have discussed providing oversight and regulations. However, if churches were to exercise long-term control, then they would likely perpetuate the past oppressive colonial roles of Christian churches. Consequently, churches can only provide moral leadership and pressure. Churches must be willing to freely share in the creation of these ventures and step away from them to let their new owners and operators control them.

Taxes

When establishing church-based economic enterprises, churches must also be aware of the tax implications. Therefore, it is critical that churches consult with their tax advisors before embarking on a new venture. Since churches are nonprofit organizations, they do not pay income taxes in the United States. However, churches will need to pay income taxes on any for-profit business that is owned by the church. They may owe Unrelated Business Income Tax (UBIT) on income generated by these new economic ventures. However, churches do not necessarily need to assume that they will need to pay income taxes. The Internal Revenue Service is primarily focused on whether a nonprofit organization remains focused on its mission. If a business has a "casual" link to the mission, then it may not be required to pay income taxes. For example, if a nonprofit is focused on job training, and they operate a grocery store as a job training site, then they may not have to pay UBIT on the profits from the grocery store.[172] In addition, a church would not be responsible for income taxes for the economic enterprises that they incubate. Again, churches should consult with their tax advisors since context and circumstance can make a tremendous difference in determining tax liability.

However, a for-profit business may be responsible for more than just income taxes. Some county governments in the United States are starting to collect property taxes on churches that use part of their property in for-profit businesses. For example, a for-profit daycare that operates in a church could jeopardize the church's property tax exemption. Therefore, it is the most prudent policy for churches to house nonprofit economic enterprises, rather than for-profit businesses. Nonprofit enterprises can still deliver strong positive cash flow for the church. Most of the largest hospital systems in the United States operate as nonprofits, and they are able to pay exorbitant executive compensation, while maintaining their nonprofit status. Finally, it is critically important that churches and their economic enterprises make all of the necessary government filings on time; otherwise, they risk fines and penalties. These filings are also important for the fair treatment of all employees and all vendors that work with the church-based economic enterprise.

Insurance

Churches also need to be aware of their insurance needs when they help to start an economic enterprise on their property. It is best for churches to use a professional licensed insurance broker to assess their risks. The insurance coverage for the church property will probably not be sufficient to cover a new economic venture, particularly a for-profit venture. Therefore, a church should take advantage of risk assessment tools to fully understand the implications of a new venture. The church's vestry or governing board must also be advised on the risks of a new enterprise and the associated insurance costs. When a church starts an economic enterprise, it should get certificates of insurance from new contractors or other vendors that are coming onto the property to serve the new business. It is also prudent to develop written policies that articulate the boundaries between the church and the church-based economic enterprises.[173]

Personnel

Like any other business, a church-based economic enterprise needs to develop a human resource strategy. Outside consultants, particularly those who are members of the church sponsoring the new venture, can be valuable resources. The human resource strategy must include planning for new hires, a detailed screening and interview process, and documentation of the process. The church should also be aware of the Workers' Compensation requirements for all employees hired by the new venture, as well as any health insurance requirements.[174] Through this process, churches and new ventures should be assured of meeting all legal compliance requirements, and they can strive to bring diversity, equity, and inclusion into the hiring process.[175]

Communications

Finally, a church needs an internal and an external communications strategy to describe the new venture that it is forming. Honest, open, and consistent communication shows respect and inclusion. It also demonstrates listening by the leaders.[176] Frequently, communication in church requires multiple venues because people generally do not pay close attention to church communication. It will also be important to post meeting minutes and to regularly update the entire congregation.

Practical theology relies upon an interdisciplinary approach. An interdisciplinary approach is also necessary to understand all of the implications of church-based economic enterprises. This chapter has explored five fields of relevant academic literature. First, it has reviewed Christian theologians' views of the global economy to frame the question of whether church-based economic enterprises can contribute to the conversation. Second, it has offered a critique of the prosperity gospel, and to a lesser extent, Business as Mission. Third, it has investigated economic alternatives for churches, and the impact of those alternatives on mission, social justice, and economic sustainability, including consideration of church planting, redemptive entrepreneurship, and asset-based community development (ABCD).[177] Fourth, it has explored the decolonial potential that these new economic enterprises can offer in a global economy plagued by legacy colonialism. Fifth, it has reviewed the practical considerations necessary in starting a church-based enterprise, including tax planning, hiring, and communications. There is guidance for churches considering the prospect of starting an economic enterprise. This guidance can direct their discernment so that they develop decolonial enterprises, advance social justice, promote economic sustainability, spur congregational growth, and ultimately, advance the *missio Dei*.

CHAPTER 2

Case Studies

To evaluate how missional and financial models can work together, this book investigates four case studies: The Church of the Messiah in Detroit; St. Peter's Evangelical Church of Christ in Louisville, Kentucky; Grace in Action Lutheran Church in Detroit; and St. Peter's Episcopal Church in Dartmouth, Massachusetts. All four case studies presented exemplify how missional models and financial models can reinforce each other while also promoting racial and social justice. In the cases selected, churches have developed economic enterprises that generate positive cash flow for the church and have an even greater economic impact on the surrounding community. Each church has taken a different approach to developing economic enterprises, and yet they have all been highly effective. The Church of the Messiah has largely incubated businesses in its facilities and supported entrepreneurs in business creation. St. Peter's Evangelical has developed a piece of property, which now houses local businesses. Grace in Action has focused on incubating business cooperatives. St Peter's Episcopal developed its own nonprofit, which now generates meaningful cash flow. Because of the diversity of these approaches, it has been critical in the research phase of this project to identify the church influences when conducting the case study. To access, understand, and document the impact of these economic enterprises within the four case studies, I have conducted extensive interviews.

The church leaders, who provided the primary input, may have a vested interest in highlighting the positive benefits to the congregation and community. Therefore, I completed additional interviews to obtain neutral inputs to supplement the qualitative data from the church leaders. As a methodology, case studies have been helpful because the church-based economic enterprises operate within clear boundaries and examine specific systems, programs, and events.[1]

The case study selection required extensive initial research about the churches and their economic ventures. Initially, cases from around the world were investigated. When selecting cases, it was critically important to have access to the leadership of the church and the economic enterprises, as well as access to individual members of the congregations. There are a number of intriguing church-based economic enterprises in Africa that are worthy of study and analysis, but the logistics of studying those cases were difficult for me because of my North American location.

The case studies were also informed by multiple sources of information, including management and employee interviews, board member and church leader interviews, business documentation, and financial statements. As a result, this book offers detailed descriptions of these enterprises. It also provides an in-depth understanding of the most successful practices of those enterprises, as well as the impact that these enterprises are having on the congregation and the surrounding community.

These case studies also highlight the importance of storytelling for historically marginalized communities. These new missional and financial models have few precedents. In addition, they have been advanced by nondominant communities that have not always had the resources to readily tell their stories and demonstrate how missional and financial models can support each other. Within critical race theory, storytelling has been an important tool in sharing the wisdom and learning that has not been included in traditional Western academia. The French philosopher Jean-François Lyotard has documented the particularly critical role of storytelling for historically marginalized and oppressed communities.[2] This book has been heavily dependent upon in-person and telephone interviews where I have listened to people's stories and then followed up on them.

While case studies have been critically important in this project, they do have limitations. Poling and Miller acknowledge that despite best efforts, descriptions are never fully adequate because the description itself is impacted by context and by the observer.[3] Context includes personal history, primary relationships, reference groups, culture, gender, and minority or majority social and economic power.[4] As a result, this work attempts to identify the context and how it may impact the interpretations and conclusions offered by this book. With critical reflection, it is still possible to garner helpful guidance from these case studies. They offer lessons in missional renewal, congregational growth, social justice, and financial sustainability.

These case studies were also not anonymous. There is increased emphasis on maintaining the privacy and anonymity of research subjects. In the past, there have been privacy violations in research projects. In addition, the research can be biased when the subjects are known by all who read the research.[5] In the case studies in this book all of the subjects were willing to discuss their congregations publicly. All had been profiled in the news media, if not in academic research, prior to this project. Ultimately, it was important that these case studies were not anonymous because their stories can be a source of inspiration for others. They have been part of the storytelling tradition described above, which has been a powerful means of conveying wisdom. These stories tell of individual and communal agency, and by telling them, others may discover that they, too, have a right to economic agency.

DOING WELL BY DOING GOOD: THE CHURCH OF THE MESSIAH, DETROIT

The Church of the Messiah (CM) is an Episcopal church in the Islandview neighborhood of Detroit. Like many inner-city churches, CM had flourished for decades in its neighborhood, but in the early 1990s, CM started to falter. Members moved out of the neighborhood and attendance started to decline. While CM was still supported by tithes and contributions, its leadership could see that change was imminent. With declining membership and shrinking contributions, CM needed a new missional focus and also a new financial model. Somewhat by accident, CM started to incubate local businesses. While the business incubator created a little revenue for the church, it was far more important for giving church and community members the confidence and resources to start new businesses that supported themselves and their community.

CM serves the Islandview neighborhood on the Eastside of Detroit, which encompasses Wayne County Census tract 5153 and Wayne County Census tract 5164. In tract 5153, 40.8% of the population lives below the poverty line, and in tract 5164, 15.5% of the population lives below the poverty line. Both tracts have far higher levels of poverty than the national average, which averages 13% of a census tract. The median income is $18,325 for tract 5153, and $43,984 for tract 5164, compared to the median national income of $69,000.[6] In tract 5153, 56.3% of the renters pay over 30% of their household income in rent, while that percentage is 58% in tract 5164. In tract 5153, 7.1% of the population does not have health insurance, while that percentage is 14.8% in tract 5164. Nationally, 9% of the population does not have health insurance. In tract 5153, 19.8% of the population does not have access to the internet, while the percentage is 23.5% in tract 5164. Both fall short of the national average of just 10% of the population without internet access. CM also sits in zip code 48205, which has the second-highest murder rate in the country.[7] Interestingly, CM has not had a murder in its congregation since 2008, and it has become a national leader in gun violence prevention through its "Silence the Violence" campaign.

CM was founded in 1824 as St. Paul's Episcopal Church, which was the first Episcopal and first Protestant church in the Michigan territory.[8] It originally stood on Woodward Avenue in downtown Detroit, but in 1851, it was moved to the corner of West Congress Street and

Shelby Street in downtown Detroit. In the new location, architect Calvin Otis built a large new church for the growing Episcopal community. St. Paul's eventually became the local Episcopal cathedral, the Cathedral Church of St. Paul. In the nineteenth century, People's State Bank designed a large new building at the corner of West Fort Street and Shelby Street. After the new bank's completion in 1901, Otis's church was moved brick by brick to CM's current location at the corner of East Grand Boulevard and Lafayette Street East, where it has stood for over a century. Soon after it was moved, the Episcopal Church in Michigan began constructing a new cathedral. Once the new cathedral was completed, the relocated St. Paul's Church was renamed the Church of the Messiah. CM has been active in its neighborhood for over one hundred years.[9]

In 1978, CM formed Church of the Messiah Housing Corporation (CMHC) to address the deteriorating housing stock in the Islandview neighborhood.[10] Now, CMHC owns over two hundred units of affordable housing. CMHC operates out of CM's campus, and CMHC pays modest monthly rent to CM, which helps to offset church expenses. More important, CMHC draws nonmembers onto the church property during the week. When people come to CMHC to apply for an apartment, they see all of the other things that are going on at CM. These activities pique their curiosity about CM, and in many cases, they return to check out the worship services on Sunday.[11] CMHC demonstrates one way that nonprofit operations can help offset the costs of a congregation while advancing mission and congregational growth.

In 1994, based on CMHC's success, the CM leadership team created BLVD Harambee (BLVD), a 501(c)(3) nonprofit corporation formed to offer social services in its Islandview neighborhood.[12] Over time, the CM leaders envisioned that BLVD might also provide financial support for the staff and facilities at CM. BLVD also attracts people to CM's campus. Like CMHC, BLVD also covers expenses related to its use of CM's building and facilities. BLVD stands for "Building Leaders for Village Development," and "Harambee" means "all pull together" in Swahili.[13] CM is centrally located in Islandview. It is geographically and missionally well-suited to serve the whole community and help the community to "all pull together." After BLVD was formed, the congregation and leadership spent several years discerning BLVD's mission. As originally conceived, BLVD was developed to provide social services, but its mission has expanded dramatically, and it now includes new business formation and development, job training, and community organizing.[14] BLVD was also organized because CM leadership realized that private foundations are reluctant to support the work of a church, even when that missional work has far-reaching secular benefits in the community. However, those same foundations would support a private nonprofit organization that was doing precisely the same work. Today, because of its strong track record, BLVD is supported by a variety of private philanthropic foundations, including the Ford Foundation and the Kellogg Foundation.

When Pastor Barry Randolph came to CM in 2002, he relied on the work of ABCD to guide the congregation in an asset assessment to determine the gifts that existed within the congregation. Due to CM's long presence in the community, BLVD had the advantage of an intimate understanding of its community.[15] CM and BLVD understood the needs, the employment trends, and the demographics of its neighborhood. They also understood the importance of addressing an immediate problem with existing resources, so that it could develop what community development pioneer Mihailo Temali has termed a "catalytic" or "symbolic" project.[16] Consistent with Mark Elsdon's advice, they decided to simply do something, even though they were uncertain about all of the details of their project. Their initial work did not need to be a major project, but it needed to build confidence in the missions of CM and BLVD. It needed to be a perceivable win, granting them a degree of credibility and visibility.[17] It needed to give CM and BLVD a sense of agency to help members and the community develop their senses of agency.

BLVD began by focusing on one of CM's most underutilized assets, its gymnasium. CM has a large gym that was not being used very often. The church also had an active member who was a basketball coach. Many of the young people in the neighborhood wanted to play basketball after school. Therefore, after evaluating its assets, CM started an after-school youth basketball program. Over time, as the coach developed strong relationships with the young people, he recognized that many of them had great potential if they could secure a formal education. Therefore, he worked with CM's leadership to develop a scholarship program for the young people in the basketball program. Many of CM's basketball players went on to college, and to professional careers that would not have been possible without higher education. CM helped them to develop the sense of agency and power to pursue higher education and all the benefits that go along with it.

After the success of the basketball program, CM started an after-school computer lab. Pastor Wally Gilbert had an extensive career in high technology before joining CM's staff. He developed a program to teach young adults how to build computers.[18] Ultimately, this program led to another scholarship program for young students who were interested in technology.[19] The computer lab has also become a resource for people in the neighborhood who are looking for jobs. As a result, CM has partnered with Hire Michigan to provide job fairs and job resources at CM. The computer lab is obvious to visitors and offers people access to the technology necessary to pursue their own goals.

During Christmas break in 2017, Pastor Wally noticed that many young people were using the CM computer lab, even though they had built their own computers, which they left at home. Pastor Wally discovered that many of the students did not have internet access at home.[20] In 2017, 40 percent of the people in Detroit did not have home access to the internet. In 2018, the federal government funded an initiative to provide internet access to underserved communities. As part of that initiative, BLVD joined the Equitable Internet Initiative (EII) to provide internet access in its neighborhood. It also partnered with Allied Media Project to develop and fund the technical support necessary to roll out internet access to the entire neighborhood.[21]

Other programs soon followed. Pastor Barry recruited a lay leader to start a marching band at CM for youth interested in music. CM now has an eighty-four-person marching band, and a music scholarship program.[22] Over six hundred students have been active in the marching band, and over two hundred have received college scholarships for music.[23] In fact, CM's marching band program has produced so many students interested in music that those students have gone on to teach music in the Detroit public schools, which had largely abandoned its music programs, because the schools could not find enough qualified teachers. Now, partially because of CM's music program, Detroit has revitalized its music programs.[24] CM also started a Christian radio station, I Am Detroit, which trains young adults in broadcasting. Students run an "unapologetically Christian" radio show, in which people can talk about the gospel openly.[25] In meeting with members of CM, I met two young men who have started media businesses as a result of their experience and training at I Am Detroit. As a result of these and other programs, CM and BLVD have helped to transform the Islandview neighborhood. CM and BLVD did not start out with a specific goal in mind. One program simply led to another and then to another. CM and BLVD did the critical work of introducing the initial programs. The whole community has benefited from these programs. Community members reported a new sense of optimism and dignity in Islandview because of CM's commitment to everyone in this part of Detroit.

During its initial asset assessment in 2002, CM identified six social workers in the congregation who could be a resource to the community. Over time, CM has also encouraged doctors, lawyers, and accountants in their congregation to tithe their time and talent to BLVD, as well. The entire CM leadership team stresses the importance of encouraging people to consider tithing time and talent. The church does not collect a lot of money from financial tithing. In fact, the 2020–2022 financial statements below show that 26 percent or less of CM's revenue comes from tithing. Nevertheless, CM is still able to do amazing missional work in its community because of the time and talent of its members and its leadership team.

Over time, CM and BLVD started to use their assets to help people start their own businesses. The church did not start BLVD with the goal of creating a business incubator; the initial goal was simply to help church and community members. The first business that CM/BLVD incubated was Nikki's Ginger Tea. Monique Sasser had developed a delicious ginger tea, and she wanted to sell it commercially.[26] She was a single mother at the time, and she did not know how to turn her tea recipe into a business. Pastor Barry and CM did not know anything about starting a beverage company either, but they helped her to develop her business nonetheless. First, Sasser needed a commercial kitchen in which to produce her tea. CM figured out how to convert its standard church kitchen into a commercial kitchen. CM then leased the commercial kitchen to Sasser at a rate well below market rates. Sasser ultimately moved to her own commercial kitchen, but CM continues to rent its kitchen to community members. Over time, the kitchen has been a critical resource in the neighborhood. It has produced ongoing revenue for CM. More important, it has been an ongoing resource for the community.

As Nikki's Ginger Tea started to sell commercially, Sasser learned that the product needed to be shelf-stable ready to sell in large grocery stores. At the time, Pastor Barry was on the board of the Center for Community-Based Enterprise (C2BE), which is developing worker-owned cooperatives in Michigan. Through C2BE, Nikki's Ginger Tea partnered with the Zingerman's Community of Businesses, which operates a series of food-related businesses. Zingerman's worked with Sasser to ensure that Nikki's Ginger Tea was shelf-stable ready. Next, to expand with major retailers, the business needed a commercial barcode and labeling system. CM helped Sasser to secure the necessary barcoding system and to connect her company with lawyers, accountants, and other professionals to help to grow her business. Nikki's Ginger Tea operated out of CM's facilities for many years and paid monthly rent until it moved into its own building. Nikki's Ginger Tea now has over twenty years of experience making and distributing natural health beverages. It employes several people in the Islandview neighborhood, and Monique Sasser has become an inspiration for many. However, Sasser might not have launched her company without CM/BLVD.[27]

After incubating the tea company, CM was approached by a church member who wanted to start a candle company. None of the leaders at CM knew anything about the candle business, but CM provided the initial space for that business, and the candle company still rents space for three days per week from CM. When another CM member wanted to start a clothing line, the church worked with the member to refine the business plan and then purchased the sewing machines and a screen press that were necessary for the clothing production. Ultimately, CM also helped the clothing line to secure a rent-free retail space in downtown Detroit. CM has also helped young people start their own businesses. Currently, the church houses two thrift stores that are run by three young men aged ten, thirteen, and fourteen. They started the thrift stores during the pandemic, and they continue to run them from CM.[28]

Overall, CM has incubated eighteen different companies that are now thriving in Islandview. All of them started at CM. Most have paid very little money directly to CM, but CM has benefited from their success. Currently, there are two new businesses that are incubating at CM.[29] All of these businesses are owned by their founders. CM does not have any control over them. In conversations with these business owners, they have a clear sense of agency, and they attribute their business success to the ministries at CM. More important, everyone at CM appreciates the benefits of these businesses to the community, even if they did not start their own businesses. At CM, the congregants refer to the church's approach to business incubation as "righteous economics."[30] As word spread about the success of CM and BLVD, BLVD started applying for grants to fund its various programs. These grants help to offset the costs of operating the church and its large physical building plant and campus. The grants are one of the reasons that CM can operate with less than 26% of its revenue coming from tithing from individual church members. The success of BLVD has also inspired what church members call "spiritual activism." They feel confident that they can put their faith into action. They know that they can be part of the *missio Dei.*

Through its community engagement, BLVD partners with Allied Media Projects to offer internet access for the Islandview neighborhood. They also partner to offer job training for local community members who are interested in becoming internet technicians, which BLVD calls "digital ministers."[31] After working with BLVD, many "digital ministers" have secured even higher-paying jobs with the major internet providers, including Xfinity, AT&T, and Spectrum. In fact, Pastor Wally maintains that his training program is far more extensive than those of the major companies.[32] As a result, the carriers are eager to hire his technicians. Those positions can pay as much as fifty dollars per hour. BLVD was such a natural partner for EII and Allied Media because it already had experience with customer service and management in Islandview through CMHC. It already had been given access to many people's homes. It was already a trusted member of the community. As a result, CM and BLVD are doing more than bringing free internet to their low-income neighbors. They are also providing technical job training, employment, and livable wages for their community.[33] The neighbors appreciate all these benefits of CM's ministry, and they are carrying those benefits with them as they also strive to make life better for their neighbors in the community.

CM's focus on innovative programs and mission has resulted in an alternative financial model. As the financial statement in figure 2.1 demonstrates, CM receives only a small portion of its revenue from tithes and offerings. In 2020, tithes and offerings were 26% of revenue, but they dropped to just 2.4% in 2021 and 5.5% in 2022. Tithing was an exceptionally low percentage of the budget in 2021 and 2022, because the church received a massive insurance settlement for terrible flood damage that occurred in 2019 and 2020. Therefore, 2021 income was positively impacted by flood insurance. The costs of the repairs after the flood were $526,701. Restoration expenses continued in 2022. There was $357,538 in 2022 building and grounds income from flood insurance, and $299,739 in building restoration expenses that were also related to the flood.

	Jan - Dec 20
Ordinary Income/Expense	
Income	
Any Need	89,442.23
loose plate	423.00
Messiah Housing Income	4,500.00
Tithes/Offerings	32,875.43
Total Income	127,240.66
Expense	
Administrator Salary	26,064.00
Apportionment	2,500.00
Cable bill	719.88
Church Alarm System	778.00
Church Insurance	16,238.00
Copier Expense	1,304.52
Dental Insurance	606.00
Dumpster expense	2,424.00
Emergency Credit Card	3,600.00
Gas & Electric Bills	20,092.00
Health Insurance	1,008.00
Office & Cleaning Supplies	2,556.00
Payroll Expenses	3,300.00
Stipends	12,800.00
Telephone Expense	4,056.32
Water Bill	6,640.06
Total Expense	104,686.78
Net Ordinary Income	22,553.88
Net Income	22,553.88

Figure 2.1. Church of the Messiah 2020 Profit & Loss Statement.
Source: Church of the Messiah, Detroit.

For 2020 through 2022, CM's tithes and offerings ranged from $24,645 to $32,875, which is well below the amount necessary to support any church operation, let alone a church as large as CM, which runs operations on approximately $100,000 per year. Expenses are so low because the clergy do not take a salary from the church. CM only has one part-time employee, the parish administrator. As a result, overall personnel expenses were only 23% of revenue in 2020, and even lower in 2021 and 2022, as seen in figures 2.2 and 2.3. Typically, churches spend closer to 50% of revenue on personnel. In a July 2022 survey of 3,000 churches, *ChurchSalary* found that churches averaged 49.1% of their revenue on salaries, while larger churches spent closer to 60%.[34] Despite exceptionally low personnel costs, CM still has other typical church expenses, including insurance, copying and printing, and building maintenance.

CM does not have a major endowment or investment fund to underwrite its expenses. Instead, the church demonstrates that alternative revenue sources are available to creative churches

	Dec 31, '20 - Dec 31, 21
Ordinary Income/Expense	
Income	
Any Need	**134,668.58**
Flood Damage/Bldg & Grounds	**868,984.16**
Kathie Von Schwarz Fund	**2,435.00**
Tithes/Offerings	**24,644.96**
Total Income	**1,030,732.70**
Expense	
A T & T	**4,941.82**
Administrative fees	**2,260.00**
Administrator Salary	**26,064.00**
Apportionment	**2,000.00**
Automobile Insurance expense	**1,300.00**
Bank Service Charges	**303.00**
Bldg & Property Insurance	**23,974.00**
Building & Grounds expense	**3,291.90**
Building & Grounds/Restoration	**526,700.66**
Charitable Contributions	**2,400.00**
Church Alarm System	**528.00**
Comcast Cable	**960.00**
Copier Expense	**3,380.73**
Dental Insurance	**600.00**
Detroit Water & Sewage	**5,118.71**
Emergency Credit Card	**12,000.00**
Gas & Electric Bills	**16,878.00**
Harambee Funds	**35,000.00**
Health Insurance	**1,048.00**
Intuit Checks	**365.00**
Miscellaneous	**168.40**
Office & Cleaning Supplies	**3,006.26**
Pastor's Discretionary Fund	**10,400.00**
Payroll Expenses	**2,650.00**
Pushpay	**1,200.00**
Stipends	**8,150.00**
Thanksgiving Dinner Items	**300.00**
Veolia Environmental	**3,012.00**
Worker's Compensation	**400.00**
Total Expense	**698,400.48**
Net Ordinary Income	**332,332.22**
Net Income	**332,332.22**

Figure 2.2. Church of the Messiah 2021 Profit & Loss Statement.
Source: Church of the Messiah, Detroit.

that are willing to experiment with new programs and economic enterprises. For example, CM has created an "Any Need" income line, which describes revenue that comes to the church and is not restricted in any way. "Any Need" income includes grants, gifts, and donations that are unrelated to worship services. CM continues to be incredibly creative in securing revenue for its ministries and programming. Pastor Barry and the CM team embrace CM and BLVD's financial uncertainty. They do not let fear limit their mission. They let the gospel drive their mission, their vision, and even their financial model.

Since Pastor Barry's arrival, CM has seen a dramatic increase in its membership and in its average Sunday attendance (ASA). When

	Jan - Dec 22
Ordinary Income/Expense	
Income	
Any Need	144,775.00
Bldg & Grounds Restoration Inco	357,538.21
Tithes/Offerings	29,302.63
Total Income	531,615.84
Expense	
A T & T	6,220.12
Administrative fees	1,240.00
Administrator Salary	26,650.00
Apportionment	8,000.00
Automobile Expense	300.00
Automobile Insurance expense	1,067.50
Bldg & Property Insurance	17,105.00
Building & Grounds expense	12,300.00
Building & Grounds/Restoration	299,739.00
Charitable Contributions	1,500.00
Church Alarm System	606.99
Church Supplies	225.13
Comcast Cable	960.00
Conferences and Meetings	1,113.00
Copier Expense	2,138.21
Dental Insurance	396.00
DTE Energy	23,759.00
Emergency Credit Card	8,400.00
Evangelism and Special Events	500.00
Gardening expense	500.00
Harambee Funds	49,542.00
Medical Insurance	109.95
Ministry Expenses	2,042.00
Office Supplies	255.00
Pastor's Discretionary Fund	8,400.00
Payroll Expenses	2,650.00
Property Taxes	316.97
Pushpay	2,400.00
Stipends	6,575.00
Thanksgiving Dinner Items	200.00
Veolia Environmental	3,017.91
Water Bill	6,107.90
Total Expense	494,336.68
Net Ordinary Income	37,279.16
Net Income	**37,279.16**

Figure 2.3. Church of the Messiah 2022 Profit & Loss Statement.
Source: Church of the Messiah, Detroit.

Pastor Barry arrived at CM in 2002, CM had just forty members.[35] At that time, CM had an aging congregation, and it was clear that, to avoid dying, the church needed to change. Rather than passively accepting death, CM chose transformation and resurrection by adopting a new perspective. CM began experimenting with several new forms of mission and new financial models.[36] Ultimately, its missional focus led to a new financial model, as well as dramatic congregational growth. While the pandemic curtailed attendance, CM had an average Sunday attendance (ASA) of over three hundred prior to the pandemic, the majority of whom were African American men under forty.[37] Currently, 60 percent of CM's members are

African American men in their thirties, and 70 percent of all members are under thirty-five.[38] Since the pandemic, membership has not reached prior levels, as seen in figure 2.4, but ASA is still well above 2002 levels, which is not true for the majority of Episcopal churches. In addition, CM continues to attract young people and young families.

At times, church members have questioned whether Pastor Barry's focus on incubating businesses is a distraction from his work as an Episcopal priest. He wholeheartedly rejects those criticisms. CM is working with underprivileged members of the neighborhood who would not otherwise have a chance to start their own businesses. Pastor Barry cites 1 Corinthians 4:20, which says that "The kingdom of God depends not on talk but on power." Pastor Barry posits that CM and BLVD are giving people power over their lives. In interviews with church and community members, I also heard consistently that people had an enhanced sense of personal and financial agency because of CM's ministries.

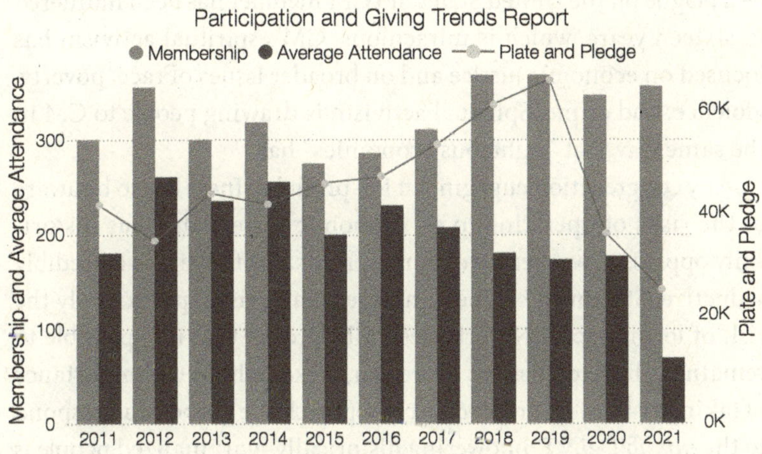

Figure 2.4. Church of the Messiah Membership, Attendance, and Giving Trends.

Source: Episcopal Church Research and Statistics, https://www.generalconvention.org/explore-parochial-report-trends.

Pastor Barry also observes that Jesus performed most of his miracles and conducted the majority of his ministry out in the community, rather than in the temple. Jesus was criticized by the temple authorities for this work, particularly when he was doing it on the Sabbath. Pastor Barry holds a similar view of those criticizing his community work, including those criticizing his ministry incubating businesses. He believes that CM is making the gospel "happen" in its community.[39] Pastor Wally points out that CM and BLVD call their community center an "inpowerment" center, because they are putting the people in the community "in power."[40] In focus groups with aspiring entrepreneurs at CM, they confirmed the "inpowerment" that they have experienced at CM. After watching other members start businesses, they realized that they could too.

More important, the "inpowerment" has led to "spiritual activism" at CM. In 2008, three young men from CM were murdered. Their deaths prompted CM to start "Silence the Violence" marches and an ongoing "Silence the Violence" campaign. What started at CM has developed into a national organization.[41] Since 2008, there have been no more murders within CM. While gun violence continues to be a plague on the United States, no CM member has been murdered in sixteen years, which is miraculous. CM's spiritual activism has focused on economic justice and on broader issues of race, poverty, violence, and crime. Spiritual activism is drawing people to CM in the same way that "righteous economics" has.[42]

Any congregation engaging in for-profit business has to be aware of the risks of operating in an economic system that has historically oppressed workers to enhance profits. Profits can be incredibly seductive. Starting a business involves many risks, particularly the risk of losing focus. Nevertheless, CM proves that it is possible to remain faithful to mission. Moreover, it exemplifies the importance of taking risks to resurrect churches, preach the gospel, and respond to the *missio Dei*.[43] Empowering historically marginalized people is one of the best ways to start to dismantle unjust economic systems of oppression. Elizabeth Liebert correctly notes that historically marginalized individuals "function as the proverbial canary in the coal mine."[44] Their lives highlight where the injustice and suffering are in a system, particularly an economic system.

Some critics worry that replicating CM's mission requires church leaders to have business experience. Pastor Barry rejects that idea completely. He points out that he knew nothing about making tea or selling candles when he helped to start those businesses, but the members of his congregation did. People who have started businesses at CM also say that Pastor Barry does not do the work for them; he does everything that he can to assist them, but ultimately, the success of the business relies upon them.[45] CM facilitates their individual agency, which is a significant benefit, because generally the current economic systems do not provide any agency for impoverished and marginalized people.

A thorough asset assessment will reveal community resources. Leaders are called to encourage congregants to share their talents and time within the community. Then, leaders must work together. CM exemplifies the value of shared distributive leadership. Their partnerships with members of the congregation and the community are enabling CM and the Islandview neighborhood to flourish and thrive. But leaders need to make the initial move. They need to be willing to try something new, and as CM demonstrates, one thing can lead to the next thing. Soon, a church can be leading a massive enterprise, even though the leadership may not have much experience with business or large organizations.

CM also formed Project I Am, which helps other churches in Michigan to assess and to use their assets. CM collaborates with 114 churches and hosts monthly meetings in which experts offer guidance.[46] For example, one month, the Michigan Department of Agriculture presented to Project I Am on how to turn a church kitchen into a commercial kitchen. Another month, the Detroit Land Bank Authority presented information about land ownership and home ownership opportunities. Through this effort, CM is expanding its missional work to the entire Michigan faith community. CM has effectively replaced an ecclesiastic understanding of the body of Christ with a missiological one. As a result, CM is serving a community that is far larger and more extensive than its congregation in Islandview. More important, it is helping that community to see the ways in which they can have collective and individual agency to address their concerns and advance the *missio Dei*.

Pastor Barry and the other clergy staff do not receive a regular paycheck from CM. Pastor Barry lives in CM's rectory for free, and he makes most of his personal income from speaking engagements, sharing the inspirational story of CM, CMHC, and BLVD.[47] There may be an understandable concern about conflicting roles in a church with several different economic ventures. Roles can certainly get confused, so there is a need for clear definitions of roles and responsibilities. Accountability is necessary for all parties. However, CM and BLVD demonstrate that this approach is viable and ultimately successful. With clear understanding of which activities are covered by CM and which are covered by BLVD, both organizations flourish, and their successes have had an undeniably positive impact on Islandview and the Eastside of Detroit.

Nevertheless, there are potential challenges. So far, BLVD has not objected to a business plan that sought its support. However, there may come a time when there is a controversial business idea that challenges CM's moral standards or presents practical limitations. CM will need to carefully discern how it continues to offer moral formation and leadership, while not applying patriarchal power that denies a person's agency.

One of the primary reasons for the success of CM and BLVD is the leadership team's deep commitment to faith. CM's Senior Warden Tamika Hamilton describes CM and BLVD as organizations that are compelled to act boldly and to be moved by the Holy Spirit.[48] Pastor Barry regularly reminds CM and BLVD that Jesus acted boldly, and we are called to act boldly as well. He reminds congregants that Christians believe that a virgin had a baby; so, Christians believe that all things are possible.[49] There is always a spiritual component to all the work at CM and BLVD. Bible study and faith formation help people to grow in their faith as they grow in the community. Pastor Barry offers impromptu Bible study after many Sunday services, which attracts many of CM's younger members.[50] In citing the importance of Scripture, Pastor Wally points out that "you can't know God's will if you don't know God's Word."[51] Pastor Barry and Pastor Wally are absolutely clear about their commitment to the Christian faith, mission, traditions, and Scriptures.

Neither Pastor Barry nor Pastor Wally are lifelong Episcopalians. Both men ultimately joined the Episcopal Church because of the mission at CM. Both men say that they had sworn off organized religion when they first discovered CM. Pastor Barry first came to CM with his mother on a Sunday because she was preaching. While he enjoyed his mother's sermon, he was disappointed in the traditional Episcopal service. Nevertheless, he saw that CM was trying to do positive things in the neighborhood, and he could see that people were responding to CM's work. Pastor Barry notes that there are approximately 4,000 churches in Detroit, but very few are actively engaged in mission in the community. CM's mission drew Pastor Barry to the church, and ultimately, to ordination. Pastor Wally had been a leader in the Progressive Baptist Convention, a predecessor of Dr. King's Southern Christian Leadership Conference. Like Pastor Barry, he was drawn to CM by its strong sense of mission. Even though CM's missional work was modest at the time that both men came to CM, it was still powerful enough to draw them to the church, and they have accelerated CM's mission.

At first, Pastor Barry and the leadership team faced resistance from some existing congregants. Not everyone was pleased with their focus on mission, rather than traditional Episcopal worship. However, they withstood the resistance because the leadership team had carefully discerned about the need for change. They seriously discerned about where God was calling them, and they acted in response to God's call. And yet, CM did not reach complete consensus. Pastor Barry cautions against paying too much attention to incumbent voices. Those views, he argues, are typically looking nostalgically to the past. He observes that when leaders ask current members for their solutions going forward, they are usually asking the wrong people. He believes that "you cannot ask people who do not have the answer for the answer."[52] If those individuals had answers, then the church would presumably not be in need of a new vision forward.[53] Leaders need to have boldness and conviction. Pastor Barry argues that people do not reject God; they reject the packaging of God offered by most churches.[54] Churches need to offer new packaging and new leadership. In the same way that a failing business changes CEOs and a failing team changes coaches, churches need to be willing to change ineffective leaders when they are failing.

CM and BLVD have not simply implemented a fresh strategy; they have created a new culture with a deep missional focus and a strong sense of personal agency. During conversations with CM and BLVD leaders and members, they repeatedly highlighted the sense of belonging that has emerged in the community. One CM member said that CM provides connections: connections to the community, connections to other aspiring entrepreneurs, connections to political leaders, connections to support, connections to services, and ultimately, connections to God.[55] When people are part of a BLVD program, they are also part of the church and vice versa. Hamilton described it as a holistic approach to work and faith. When Pastor Barry meets with new members of CM and BLVD, he sets the expectation that they will "pay it forward," and give back to the CM/BLVD communities.[56] One congregant told the story of how he arrived at CM on his first Sunday, and Pastor Barry immediately put him to work moving boxes out of storage. Pastor Barry sets the expectations that all are called to this work together, and now members expect that of each other.[57] They expect to find support at CM. They expect to be seen as a child of God, made in the image and likeness of God.

After observing their work, professor and congregational development specialist David Kresta calls the work of CM a "holistic community engagement."[58] CM seriously considers its impact on "the community ecosystem to drive long-term and sustainable community change," even if they do not use that language.[59] Pastor Barry has moved past a dichotomy of spiritual and secular to bring the gospel to life through the actions and faith of CM and the surrounding neighborhood.[60] Pastor Barry refers to all this as the "Messiah Effect." He has seen the profound effect that the Church of the Messiah is having in his community.

When incubating companies, CM does not provide seed capital, but they do provide critical support and encouragement. Some of the businesses pay rent to the church, which aids its financial model. More important, however, several of these businesses have moved out of the church and into their own spaces, where they can hire more people, expand their business, and demonstrate the "Messiah Effect."

CM and BLVD provide more than charity and social services for the Islandview neighborhood and the Eastside of Detroit; they are advancing social justice by reducing economic and racial inequality. CM and BLVD are empowering community members to develop their own businesses, to live in their own apartments, and to have their own internet access. They have actively worked to develop networks within the neighborhood and to organize the broader community, and they have developed innovative ways to do both. CM and BLVD have also been effective advocates for their neighborhood. CM has been casting a vision and providing encouragement to other churches that seek to promote change and transformation through business enterprises. Pastor Barry's charismatic leadership inside and outside of CM has been evangelistic and inspirational. No matter what the challenge, Pastor Barry and CM are not easily deterred. Pastor Barry says, "Whatever excuse you got, we got a solution."[61] He says, "Everything is an opportunity. Everything is an opportunity for greatness."[62]

CM is truly an "intersectional church," working to address the myriad ways in which prejudice, racism, and exploitation seek to keep people marginalized, oppressed, and powerless.[63] CM exemplifies a commitment to its congregation, community, and historically marginalized members. It is building an institution that addresses both "America and God's hunger for kin-dom on earth defined by God's idea of justice and peace."[64]

CM demonstrates several critical features for churches considering alternative financial models:

1. **The primary focus must be missional, not financial.** CM and BLVD prove that a missional focus can generate the resources necessary to operate church ministries. CM did not try to start a business incubator. It simply tried to help a member of the church start a new business, and over time, a business incubator has emerged.
2. **A clergy person does not need a business background or entrepreneurial experience to start new businesses.** Rather, a clergy leader needs to be willing to conduct an honest asset assessment of the congregation. The asset assessment process enabled the leaders at CM to identify the resources, particularly the human talent, in their midst. For CM, one important asset was the individuals who wanted to start businesses. Not every congregation has budding entrepreneurs, but those who do might try to foster that talent. Once entrepreneurs emerged at CM, BLVD relied upon them to lead new businesses. Research suggests that entrepreneurs do not need any special skills, but they need a willingness to try new things and to learn from failures.[65]
3. **Leaders need to be committed for the long term.** Pastor Barry has been serving CM for over twenty years, and he has spent much of that time also leading BLVD as its executive director. In addition, Senior Warden Tamika Hamilton has served at CM for decades. Transforming a missional and economic model takes patience and time. Leaders must develop the self-care and support necessary to remain committed, even in the face of setbacks and delays.
4. **All leaders must be willing to experiment with new models of mission, as well as new models of church finance.** CM has started dozens of programs, and the church is constantly partnering with other organizations. The leadership teams are not intimidated by experimentation or afraid of failure. They have realistic expectations, and they are willing to discontinue a program or policy if it

is not working for the community. Currently, CM is contemplating how it can use its extensive experience in the neighborhood to stop gun violence in Detroit. Overall, CM demonstrates that churches can no longer work only through their traditional channels and venues.[66] The *missio Dei* calls upon churches to try new ways of serving God and the community.

5. **Active lay leadership is essential.** CM's 2002 asset assessment was almost entirely based on the talent of the 40 people who were attending CM when Pastor Barry started as its rector. He did not develop all these businesses and programs on his own. They are the fruit of multiple partnerships within the community. These ventures needed support, and CM offered it freely.
6. **Mission emerges from supporting people on the margins.** CM provides support for people who have little to no opportunities in the current economic systems. No one else was ready to help a single mother start a business or to help a recently incarcerated person find housing and a job. As part of the *missio Dei*, CM creates economic opportunities for historically marginalized people. The people of CM and the surrounding neighborhood are well aware of their economic challenges and the bias that they face daily in the current economic system. Like other "resurrected" congregations, CM has identified ways to counteract poverty and unemployment through its Christian mission.[67]
7. **Congregations must know their local ecosystem.** CM knows its local ecosystem, and it actively partners with all sorts of individuals and organizations. CM and BLVD know the local private businesses, the local developers, the community organizations, the private foundations, and the government agencies.[68] Similarly, before starting on any new venture, it is critical that a church know its local ecosystem very well.

8. **Faith and mission must be at the center.** In all CM's work, spirituality and mission play a key role. Pastor Barry quotes Scripture as he advocates for new businesses and new programs. People attend Sunday services because of the missional work that CM is doing the rest of the week. They are not just talking about the gospel at CM; they are living it. The ministries, mission, and businesses at CM evidence the present and creative power of God. Their work has resurrected the Church of the Messiah, and it provides a model of how other churches might find their own resurrection and become a shining example of the Holy Spirit in their communities. By leading with the *missio Dei*, a healthy financial model has followed. A financial challenge does not need to be a reason for despair; it can be an opportunity for new mission. CM demonstrates that when prioritizing the *missio Dei*, it is possible for churches to be doing well by doing good.

IF YOU BUILD IT, THEY WILL COME: ST. PETER'S UNITED CHURCH OF CHRIST AND THE VILLAGE @ WEST JEFFERSON

Many churches rent out their property. In fact, some churches, like Trinity Episcopal Church in New York City, generate millions of dollars annually in passive rental income. A growing number of churches are starting to develop their property, and many are hoping to provide affordable housing. Few churches, however, develop their real estate into facilities that foster ongoing economic development in their communities. St. Peter's Evangelical United Church of Christ (SP) in Louisville, Kentucky, is a church that did just that. SP is an exemplary model of doing well by doing good through missional real estate development. SP demonstrates that the *missio Dei* can happen in any market at any time. In 2022, SP and its nonprofit community development corporation

MOLO Village (MV) broke ground on The Village @ West Jefferson (VWJ), which is a two-story, 30,000-square foot facility that houses a health clinic, a credit union, a nonfranchise restaurant, a business incubator, and several other local small businesses, as seen in figure 2.5. VWJ cost over $7 million dollars to develop, and it represented the first major investment in its neighborhood in decades. SP's journey to developing VWJ was not quick or easy to build, but it illustrates how a new missional model can build new financial sustainability. Moreover, in doing this missional work, SP has given its community new hope, and it has given individuals in the neighborhood a new sense of personal agency. They see that new developments can occur in their neighborhoods, and more important, in their lives.

SP was founded in 1857 on the west side of Louisville, and its current facility was completed in 1895. Located in the Russell neighborhood, it sits directly across the street from what had been Beecher Terrace, the largest affordable housing community in Jefferson County, Kentucky. Beecher Terrace had over 760 units. It was originally constructed as public housing in the 1930s, and it is in the process of being converted to mixed-use affordable housing. In 2014, the original buildings were demolished. As a result, between

Figure 2.5. Villages at West Jefferson.
Source: Molo Village CDC.

2014 and 2016, over 4,000 prior residents of Beecher Terrace were displaced and scattered around the metropolitan Louisville area. Consequently, SP experienced a dramatic drop in membership. By 2019, prior members began to return to SP. SP sits on the west side of the famous 9th Street Divide in Louisville, which has long separated east and west Louisville. Historically, the west side, unlike the east side, has seen little investment.

Originally, SP was a congregation of German-speaking immigrants, and it retained its German legacy well into the 2000s, even as the neighborhood became a more consistently African American community. When SP's current pastor, the Rev. Jamesetta Ferguson, arrived at SP in 2006, the membership consisted of 15 German senior citizens, the majority of whom were over eighty years old. Some of those members refused to worship with Pastor Ferguson because she is an African American woman.[69] Despite its legacy of racism, SP always viewed itself as a "lighthouse" to the surrounding African American community. However, that community did not view itself as part of the church. Under Pastor Ferguson's leadership, SP is now a multiethnic, multiracial, and multigenerational church. Over the last few years, it has increased its membership from approximately 50 members to 160 members.

St Peters, MOLO Village, and the Villages at West Jefferson are located in Jefferson County in census tract 2402. In this census tract, 22.4% of the population lives below the federal poverty level, which is well above the national average of 13% of the census tract living in poverty. The median income is $55,575, which is below the national average of $69,000. However, Pastor Ferguson clarified that the incomes in the Russell neighborhood are well below those levels. In 2013, when the plans began for demolition of Beecher Terrace, the average income was just $18,000.[70] While incomes have increased modestly since 2013, they are not approaching the average for the census tract. Additionally, 24.1% of renters pay over 30% of household income on housing, which is below the national average of 46%.[71] Also, 5.7% of the population has no health insurance, which is better than the national average of 9%. In this census tract, 12.9% of the population have no home internet access, which is higher than the national average of 10%. There are no grocery stores in this census tract or within 1.5 miles of SP, MV or VWJ. The closest grocery story is a Save A Lot, which is 1.6 miles away.[72] There are no hospitals or urgent care facilities in the neighborhood either. The closest urgent care center is 1.1 miles away from SP. There are not even any health clinics, despite the housing density. The closest clinics are the Park DuValle Community Health Center and the HMPS Internal Medicine Center, both of which are just under a mile away from SP. Prior to VWJ, there were only two financial institutions in this census tract, Commonwealth Credit Union and a Fifth Third Bank branch office.

Pastor Ferguson noted that when she first arrived at SP and started to consider redeveloping the property, she did not face opposition from the congregation. However, the east side business leaders were deeply skeptical and opposed the change. They had had bad experiences in the past. There had been limited investments in projects in the West End. The past attempts at redevelopment ultimately either did not meet expectations, or they were never completed.[73] There had been a lot of disappointment, and there had been no new commercial construction in the neighborhood in decades. However, Pastor Ferguson found that over time, the east side leaders recognized that growth on the west side was necessary to accommodate the burgeoning demands of downtown Louisville.[74]

In February 2011, SP formed MOLO Village CDC, a community development corporation. "Molo" means "welcome" in Xhosa, a southern African language, and VWJ is certainly a welcome addition to the Russell community. VWJ is housing the first new retail construction in the neighborhood in over thirty years.[75] It is also housing a major health institute, Norton Healthcare's Institute for Health Equity (IHE). IHE provides telehealth consultation rooms and access to prevention and wellness services.[76] The VWJ location enables Norton Healthcare to better serve the BIPOC community. IHE medical director Dr. Kelly C. McCants explains that "the premise of the institute is that health equity can be achieved only when every person has a fair opportunity to achieve their full health potential. We are committing time, talent, and resources necessary toward this essential human right" at the VWJ location.[77] The Russell neighborhood is already seeing better health outcomes since Norton's clinic has opened at VWJ. People are much more likely to visit the clinic in the neighborhood than they were to go to the emergency room, which was their only option prior to the Norton clinic. They are taking much more control and ownership of their health than they were in the past.[78] VWJ is also housing the first financial services in the neighborhood, the Park Community Credit Union. Since opening its VWJ branch, Park Community Credit Union has already made over $7.5 million in affordable home loans on the west side of Louisville.[79] The Park Community Credit Union branch manager Lisa Raines sees an opportunity to provide broader access to financial products. She says, "Opening those opportunities to people who haven't had those in the past is critical. Financial security is so important. Having someone who actually understands that and who cares can make a difference."[80] These financial services are key to closing the racial wealth divide that exists in Louisville and across the United States. Both the health care and the financial services that are available at VWJ are giving the neighbors an enhanced sense of their own agency and their own dignity. They can envision a life for themselves and their families that includes reliable health care and necessary financial services. Both had previously been a luxury in the Russell neighborhood, and now, they seem more like a right.

VWJ also houses the Russell Technology Business Incubator (RTBI). Its executive director, Dave Christopher, works with Black and Latino entrepreneurs in the neighborhood.[81] RTBI provides everything that an entrepreneur needs to succeed, including seed capital for new equipment, accounting and marketing support, web design, and software application development. Thus far, RTBI has assisted start-up local businesses in software applications, restaurants, catering, logistics, event planning, fashion design, and public speaking.[82] In addition, Christopher is bringing his existing ventures to RTBI. He has led Amped, which stands for "Adventurous Minds Produce Extraordinary Dreams." Amped uses music and technology to empower young people and their families.[83] These new business opportunities are creating greater economic equality, and they are alleviating poverty on the west side of Louisville. VWJ's mission is also deeply decolonial because it is enabling people who have historically been exploited by the current economic system to develop ownership and wealth on their own terms. It is enabling them to delink from the prior economic systems that exploited the Russell neighborhood. Empowering people who have historically been marginalized and oppressed by the current economic system is one way to start to dismantle colonial economies and develop a different economic future.

VWJ is also home to ten other new businesses, including a cooperative preschool, a Black-owned realty company, and the only nonfranchise restaurant in the neighborhood. Once fully developed, the businesses at VWJ are expected to employ one hundred people, bringing approximately $25 million to the Russell neighborhood.[84] In all their work, Pastor Ferguson has encountered very little resistance from her congregation. In fact, VWJ is bringing people to SP who would never have considered coming into a church in the past. They have witnessed SP's commitment to the neighborhood, and they have decided to worship at SP. In short, SP's missional focus through VWJ has driven congregational renewal and economic sustainability.

Through all her work, Pastor Ferguson has been inspired by her Christian faith. It is an expression of the *missio Dei.* She sees VWJ and the other social services at SP as an expression of her faith and her discipleship. She believes that God is present in this work, which is enabling SP to rebuild its surrounding community. In the past, churches were the capstones of a community. They brought the community together and held it together. However, Ferguson believes that over time, churches turned more inward. They became ecclesiologically centered, rather than missionally focused. By encouraging SP to look outside the church walls to determine where SP can bring God's loving presence more fully and visibly into the community, Pastor Ferguson has renewed SP's focus on mission, and SP has embodied the *missio Dei.*[85]

Like so many stories of new mission, SP did not start out with the ambitious goal of building a 30,000-square foot facility. Rather, Pastor Ferguson was trying to improve the living conditions in the neighborhood where she had been raised. When she returned to Russell to lead St. Peter's, she saw abundant need. She initiated partnerships with existing community organizations. The first partnership was with Dare to Care, which annually brought 4,000 lbs to 5,000 lbs of food to SP to distribute in the neighborhood. Not long after SP launched this partnership, the food pantry that had housed Dare to Care was no longer available for the organization. So, SP stepped in and offered its facilities to the program. As a result, SP now distributes over 200,000 lbs of food weekly to over 14,000 people from its facilities.[86] Moreover, it actively aims to reduce hunger in the community by teaching about nutrition and cooking. As a result, it is empowering people to overcome hunger in their midst. With a greater control over hunger and nutrition, people have been able to pursue other goals of their lives, like securing good health care, finding meaningful employment, and even starting new businesses.

Pastor Ferguson also responded to the need for a number of other social services. SP has developed extensive drug and alcohol recovery programs, as well as reentry programs for people who have recently left in-patient drug and alcohol treatment. One of the largest drug and alcohol recovery programs in the country, The Healing Place, is within a mile of SP. Many of SP's members are individuals who have participated in those programs and who continue to need support. Ferguson also observed a need for children's programs. So, SP has developed an extensive after-school program. Finally, SP has established an adult day care program for the senior citizens in its neighborhood.[87]

At the same time that SP was responding to the needs in the community, the SP's church facility needed extensive building repairs. There was a significant health risk from mold and lead. Structural repairs were estimated to cost more than $1 million. SP approached the Church Building & Loan Fund (CB&LF) for a loan. CB&LF rejected the request, but Pastor Ferguson started to meet with CB&LF

Executive Director Rev. Patrick Duggan. They began to explore other ways that SP could use its facilities to serve the neighborhood. One asset was SP's parking lot, which was underutilized. Ferguson and Duggan discussed ways to use it. SP identified several needs: health care facilities, banking facilities, a sit-down restaurant, mentoring programs, business incubators, and tools for building generational wealth through real estate. Because these needs were so pressing, SP determined that it could not merely address one of them. Therefore, the answer was to develop commercial real estate space for the businesses and organizations that could meet them all.[88] VWJ was envisioned not only as a new commercial building, but also as a resource for rebuilding the community and building up lives. It was intended to reconcile people to one another, to creation, and, ultimately, to God.

The challenges were enormous for such an ambitious project. From the beginning, it was clear that this development was going to cost millions of dollars. CB&LF worked with Ferguson, SP, and MV to articulate strategies for developing and funding VWJ.[89] Duggan calls VWJ the "most unusual project in the 167-year history" of CB&LF.[90] He also recognizes that many congregations find themselves in similar situations. They are facing dire financial straits and yet have valuable real estate assets that could expand their mission. CB&LF is showcasing VWJ's success in hopes that other congregations might also make bold attempts at real estate redevelopment and missional revival in their neighborhoods. CB&LF is also raising $100 million in additional investment capital for comparable projects.[91]

When SP first approached Louisville Mayor Greg Fischer about VWJ, he was supportive of the project. But Fischer also understood the funding challenges. As a result of Fischer's support, Louisville's economic development team worked with SP to find the necessary funds, via tax credits, foundation grants, and funding from the US Department of Housing and Urban Development (HUD).[92] Ultimately, because of the size and scope of VWJ, the project had nine sources of funding, including a $4.2 million loan from CB&LF, the Mission Investment Fund of the Evangelical Lutheran Church in America, and the Disciples Church Extension Fund; $2.2 million in equity through the purchase of $7 million in New Market Tax Credits; and $1.5 million in grants from HUD, the City of Louisville, and two local philanthropic foundations.[93] As part of securing the New Market Tax Credits, VWJ had to demonstrate how this project would serve the needs of the surrounding community. It outlined the importance of their missional work in the application, and it continues to reinforce its commitment to the *missio Dei* in its daily operations.

In the midst of the VWJ development, SP has still been addressing structural issues with its church and the $5 million of repairs that are necessary to make the church safe and habitable. Currently, the congregation is worshipping in a 5,000-square foot retail space in the Russell neighborhood. Pastor Ferguson initially expected the project to take four years to complete. Now, it looks as though ten years is more realistic, partly because the project has grown over time. SP is in the process of repurposing its sanctuary space and transforming it into space that can serve a variety of purposes. Ultimately, SP will transition from a 30,000-square foot sanctuary with seating for 1,000 to a 15,000-square foot flexible space with seating for 150 people. The new seating will not be permanently affixed to the floor, so that people can easily move the chairs to accommodate a variety of groups.

SP is also constructing an adjoining 15,000-square foot building that will house the Dare to Care program, along with a commercial kitchen, additional offices, and an event space. This new facility will also address the dire need for commercial space on the west side. SP received an additional $2 million grant in December 2022 from the City of Louisville to help fund this project. The converted space will also include a resource library, worship chapel, and other community services.[94] Even after all SP's commercial construction projects, Pastor Ferguson sees the need for three to four additional commercial buildings in the neighborhood.[95] After decades of neglect, SP is bringing basic infrastructure to the neighborhood so that the community has the tools necessary to thrive, and it appears to be working. People are using these facilities to meet their daily needs and their professional goals.

More people have been drawn to SP because they see SP's serious commitment to the community and to its mission. Even in its temporary location, between 600 to 700 people gather at SP during the week. Most of them are not coming for worship services. They come for recovery programs, nutrition training, prisoner reentry support, and the food pantry.[96] Moreover, Pastor Ferguson maintains that she offers far more ministry at VWJ during the weekdays than at the church on Sunday. While she only leads worship at SP on Sunday, she is at VWJ for the rest of the week.[97] She is extending her church's mission well outside its sanctuary walls. She is providing a contemporary vision of the *missio Dei*.

Finally, VWJ is already providing financial benefits to SP. Prior to the project, SP collected approximately $100,000 in annual tithes and financial contributions. VWJ is already adding almost $50,000 in revenue to SP.[98] Overall, VWJ is generating $75,000 to $100,000 in profits, but VWJ's board is distributing funds conservatively to SP until it has a clearer picture of long-term expenses and depreciations from the project. In addition, Pastor Ferguson is the CEO of VWJ, and she receives a salary in that position. She receives no compensation from SP at this point. VWJ is not only contributing income to SP, it is also helping to offset the costs of operating the congregation and the church. However, this is not a conflict of interest. By serving as the CEO of VWJ and the pastor at SP, Pastor Ferguson is able to ensure that the church and VWJ remain committed to their common values and mission.[99]

While SP did not embark on VWJ looking for a new financial model, it has found one. Without a major endowment or investment fund to underwrite its expenses, the church had to be creative. VWJ proves that alternative revenue sources are available to churches willing to experiment with new programs and new economic enterprises. These programs and enterprises are adapting SP's mission to the needs of the neighborhood, while remaining true to its original missional commitment of preaching and sharing the gospel of Jesus Christ. Pastor Ferguson has discovered that SP's outreach ministries are particularly powerful for young adults who want to see their church engaged with the needs of the world. For too long, churches have been more focused on activities inside their walls rather than the evangelical call to take action outside of them.[100] SP also writes grants and fundraises to support VWJ and its mission. Pastor Ferguson and the SP and MV team embraces SP and MV's financial uncertainty. They have not allowed their financial uncertainty to turn into anxiety, nor do they permit fear to limit their mission. Instead, they let the gospel drive their mission, their vision, and even their financial model.

Over the past two years, Pastor Ferguson has been sharing what she has learned from the VWJ project. She has given numerous press interviews, and CB&LF has produced a video documenting the development of VWJ. Ferguson expects to continue to share information about VWJ after she retires. As she says, "God didn't do this for me to hang onto this."[101] Ferguson recognizes that SP and VWJ can serve as models for other churches considering sustainable faith-based community development and the *missio Dei*.

Any congregation engaging in for-profit business has to be aware of the potential risks of operating in the current economic system. Liebert suggests Appreciative Inquiry (AI) as a way to move an enterprise beyond a preoccupation with its own needs to broader social needs. Based on public and private interviews with Pastor Ferguson and her team, it appears that AI has been used throughout the development process.[102] Starting a business entails many risks, particularly the risk of losing focus. Nevertheless, Pastor Ferguson and SP prove that it is possible to do so while remaining true to a mission. Moreover, their success underscores the importance of taking risks to resurrect churches, preach the gospel, and respond to God's call. In fact, their example has encouraged others in the community to take risks and to dream about different possibilities for themselves, just like SP did for itself.

Pastor Ferguson and SP live into a mission to care for the poor and marginalized that reflects their Christian faith. As Ferguson says:

> I have undertaken the transformation of a traditional congregation in urban Louisville and have led them to great success

> in reaching people in a predominantly African-American community. Creating an atmosphere of harmony and unity in this increasingly diverse society is key to helping people care about one another and a willingness to help one another. I have also served as an advocate for the people in the congregation and community to seek individual identity through spiritual growth and participation in social services that will empower them in their individual lives and families to become better men, women, and children.[103]

SP and Pastor Ferguson have demonstrated several features that are critical for churches considering alternative missional and financial models. In fact, there are eight characteristics of SP that are consistent with the Church of the Messiah in Detroit:

1. **The primary focus must be missional, not financial.** SP's initial focus was not primarily financial. SP approached CB&LF for a loan to renovate the church, but Pastor Ferguson was really focused on her neighborhood. SP did not start out looking to develop a 30,000-square foot facility but tried to get her neighbors the things that they needed: a bank, a health clinic, and jobs. SP did not shy away from an enormous challenge that forced her to work in unfamiliar fields with new people.
2. **A clergy person does not need a business background or entrepreneurial experience to start new businesses.** A clergy leader needs to be willing to conduct an honest asset assessment of the congregation. Pastor Ferguson had a business background, but she had never been a real estate developer. Through an asset assessment, Ferguson worked with Duggan and CB&LF, and they identified SP's large parking lot as an underused asset. They recognized that they were not adequately stewarding this resource, so, SP took the bold move of doing something new with the property.

3. **Leaders need to be committed for the long term.** Pastor Ferguson has been serving SP for sixteen years. She has spent over ten years working on VWJ, and her work is not done. She also had the support of Duggan, who brought his years of experience and deep commitment to the project. A similar transformation has occurred at the Church of the Messiah, where the pastor has been working at the church for over twenty years and lay leaders had demonstrated equally long-term commitments to the church.
4. **All leaders need to be willing to experiment with new models of mission, including new financial models.** Leaders need to move beyond an ecclesiological vision of church to a missional one. A willingness to experiment can also extend to the congregation and the community, who see that they, too, might experiment. Helping people to experiment is one of the most powerful forms of human agency and decoloniality.
5. **Active lay leadership is essential.** Pastor Ferguson relied upon leaders inside and outside of the church. These lay leaders also started to take greater control of their own lives, and to see the resources at VWJ as resources that were available to them to achieve their hopes and dreams.
6. **Mission emerges from supporting people on the margins.** SP provides support for people who are oppressed by the current economic systems. The church provides food and recovery programs. It supports people who were recently incarcerated. As an act of faith and mission, SP resists the current economic systems of oppression by creating economic opportunities for historically marginalized people.
7. **Congregations must know their local ecosystems.** SP knows its local ecosystem, and it actively partners with all sorts of individuals and organizations in the Russell neighborhood. It takes a holistic approach to community engagement and economic development.[104]

8. **Faith and mission must be at the center.** In all SP work, there is a consistent link to Christian faith and mission. Pastor Ferguson quotes Scripture as she advocates for new businesses and new programs. People attend Sunday services because of the missional work that SP is doing the rest of the week. Their work has resurrected St. Peter's Evangelical United Church of Christ, and it provides a model of how other churches might find their own resurrection and be a shining example of the Holy Spirit in their communities. By leading with missional work, a healthy financial model has followed. A financial challenge does not need to be a reason for despair; it can be an opportunity for new mission, just like SP. SP is demonstrating that, just like the movie *Field of Dreams* says, "if you build it, they will come." In this case, their building is bringing new jobs, new businesses, new hope, personal agency, decoloniality, and new life to their community. It is bringing the *missio Dei*.

COOPERATIVE ECONOMIC ENTERPRISES: A STUDY OF GRACE IN ACTION CHURCH COOPERATIVES

The third case study investigates missional and financial renewal in a Latino congregation. Grace in Action Church (GIA) is a Lutheran congregation that was planted by Lutheran leaders John Cummins and Meghan Sobocienski in Detroit in 2014. As part of its mission, GIA formed Grace in Action Collective (GIAC) to develop a business cooperative program within its southwest Detroit neighborhood.[105] Cooperatives are economic ventures that involve shared ownership and governance. They can include real estate or operating businesses. In GIA's case, the church has helped to launch several new business cooperatives, including a web design cooperative, a day care, a translation service, a commercial cleaning cooperative, and an apparel cooperative. When they started working with cooperatives,

GIA and its leaders knew nothing about starting them. The resulting economic enterprises have reinvigorated the local economy and the community. Exemplars like GIA are encouraging. They illustrate new forms of economic enterprise that move beyond the exploitative colonial practices of the current economic system. They provide inspiring models of "shareholding/postindustrial capitalism."[106] They demonstrate that an economic system does not need to disregard the dignity of the people who work in it. Rather, an economic system can provide equitably for workers, owners, and the entire community, whether the enterprise is structured as a cooperative business or as an individual business. More important, in interviews with people who have started these cooperatives, it is clear that GIA has given them an enhanced sense of economic agency, and they have become an inspiration to others in their community. GIA's success demonstrates that Christian churches in the United States can learn to offer local economic alternatives to economic globalism, thereby fulfilling their theological mission and their communities' economic needs. In supporting cooperatives, they can enhance the *missio Dei*.

GIA and GIAC serve neighborhoods that encompass Wayne County Census tract 5242 in southwest Detroit. In this tract, 42.7% of the population live below the poverty line, which is far higher than the national average of 13% of a census tract living in poverty.[107] The median income is $40,986, which is below the median national income of $69,000.[108] Also, 35.6% of renters pay over 30% of their household income in rent, and 45.7% of homeowners pay over 30% of their household income in mortgage payments.[109] In tract 5242, 19.7% of the population does not have health insurance.[110] Nationally, 9% of the population does not have health insurance. Finally, 16.2% of the population does not have home access to the internet, which is higher than the national average of 10%.[111] The neighborhood immediately surrounding GIA and GIAC is predominately Latino, with people from many different parts of Latin America, particularly Mexico. The neighborhood largely consists of single-family residences and single-story retail spaces. There are also some abandoned industrial sites in the community, which create some large vacant spaces. There is a surprising economic vibrancy in the neighborhood, which is usually missing from census tracts with comparable metrics.

GIA illustrates the healing power of economic development. By helping people to develop new economic enterprises, GIA is helping to heal broken economic systems and following Jesus's exhortation to preach the gospel and heal the sick. The church is embodying Jesus's resurrection in their midst by bringing new life to communities, churches, and individuals that seemed to be dead. They are showing to the world how the Mission of God can be manifest in low-income neighborhoods in the twenty-first century. The community has responded well to GIA's ministry. Everywhere one looks in the community, there is new construction and redevelopment. There are new parks and new businesses, and the members of the community have a deep sense of ownership of their community. At least partially due to GIA, the members of the community have a new sense of dignity and a new pride in their neighborhood.

Long before the rise of the current economic system, the medieval Arab Muslim scholar Ibn Khaldun recognized the importance of collaborative economic practices, like cooperatives. He introduced the concept of *asabiyya*, which loosely means "group solidarity."[112] He recognized that individuals need community and collaboration, and he specifically acknowledged the financial requirements of communal living. He understood that people need to receive fair wages, relative to the costs of living in their community. Otherwise, they might be forced to leave the community for economic reasons. If enough people left their jobs, then the entire economic sector would collapse.[113] While Khaldun was writing over six hundred years ago, his concept of *asabiyya* is a helpful corrective to the contemporary challenges of the current global economic system. He clarifies the importance of economic collaboration and a "collective spirit," which is also apparent in GIA's cooperatives.[114]

The *asabiyya* spirit has been evident in the work of Lutheran leaders John Cummins and Meghan Sobocienski, as well as the many people that have been part of their ministries, particularly those who have started cooperatives.[115] John and Meghan are trained in community organizing, and they used their organizing backgrounds to discern the needs of their neighborhood when they started Grace in Action Church. As a church plant, John and Meghan were initially financed by the Southeast Michigan Synod of the Evangelical Lutheran Church of America (ELCA). They held over one hundred one-to-one interviews with people in the neighborhood. Subsequently, they initially offered citizenship classes, guitar lessons, and community gatherings.[116]

One summer, they organized an art camp for young people. As part of the camp, they offered a silk-screening class. At the conclusion of the camp, one fourteen-year-old young man was so excited about silk-screening that he wanted to start a business. Meghan worked with him and five other young people to start a cooperative business that designs and produces silk-screened apparel. They named it Stitching Up Detroit. When the start-up cooperative needed space for production equipment, John and Meghan welcomed them into their home garage. When the cooperative outgrew the garage, Meghan worked with them to find inexpensive commercial space in the neighborhood. When they outgrew that space, Meghan and John helped Stitching Up Detroit move into a larger garage located on GIA's church property. Stitching Up Detroit now employs four to five people and produces thousands of silk-screened items every year. It is a vibrant, independent economic enterprise and strong cooperative. In fact, in 2025, Stitching Up Detroit began to pay modest rent to GIA for the use of the garage. The rent will not fund GIA's programmatic work, but it will offset some of the costs of operating its church property.[117]

When Meghan and John started working with Stitching Up Detroit, neither of them knew anything about starting a cooperative business. Nevertheless, they worked with the young entrepreneurs to find key resources at each stage of development. Subsequently, Meghan and John heard from other people in the neighborhood who were also interested in starting cooperatives.[118] They identified a compelling need for new business development in their community and responded by forming GIAC.[119] Meghan leads GIAC. In her work, she has found herself continually learning with the historically marginalized people in her community.

Over time, GIA may recognize modest revenue from their cooperative businesses, but John and Meghan do not believe that GIA's revenue will ever cover a significant part of the church's expenses. Initially, John and Meghan planned to start a business of their own, much like the church plants described by Samuel Lee. However, they understood that it typically takes seven years for a business to become profitable. Instead, they chose to help other people start businesses. John sees a symbiotic relationship between the church and the collective. The collective helps the church focus on the surrounding community, and the church helps the collective maintain a moral compass. He recognizes that churches can become too insular, and nonprofits can become too focused on internal operations. Together, the church and the collective have developed a highly collaborative venture that embodies some of the principles of *asabiyya*, as well as Paul's body of Christ theology and the *missio Dei*.

Generally, the cooperatives started at GIA are small local businesses that generate positive cash for the cooperative owners. If the church owned the businesses, then the cash flow from the businesses might cover the expenses of the church. In GIA's case, GIAC has received grant money for training people in cooperative development, and they have generated consulting fees that have helped to underwrite GIAC.[120] However, these cooperatives primarily support their employees. In this way, these businesses do not fit within the traditional understanding of a capitalist business. They do not prioritize profitability or the accumulation of capital. They consider the impact of their business on employees, shareholders, and the community.

The business cooperatives developed by GIAC represent a new way of fulfilling economic needs while addressing systemic challenges of the current economic system. These cooperatives have an opportunity to remedy some of the past injustices that have developed out of the current economic system's drive to accumulate capital. This cooperative approach may not address all the challenges of the current economic system, but it does represent a positive alternative. Moreover, these cooperatives are largely local in nature, which gives them an advantage over global competitors because they do not need to grow profits or accumulate capital. Instead, the cash flow that would have been directed toward executive compensation, profits, and capital accumulation can be applied to employee compensation and to offset the higher costs of operating locally.

While GIA has adopted a novel approach to business formation, business cooperatives are not new. The first types of business cooperatives emerged in England after the Industrial Revolution. They developed out of the trade and social guild traditions that preceded the Industrial Revolution. The first cooperative business in the United States was a mutual fire insurance company organized by Benjamin Franklin in 1752. The first dairy and cheese cooperatives in the United States were organized in 1810.[121] Cooperatives have generally risen and fallen in sync with the US economy, but they remain particularly strong in the agriculture and food sectors. Cooperatives include such well-known food-production businesses as Land O'Lakes, Welch's, Sunkist, Sun-Maid, and Ocean Spray, as well as outdoor retailer REI, and French banking giant Crédit Agricole. One of the most inspiring cooperatives is Mondragon Corporation, which was launched in Spain's Basque region in 1956. In building its cooperative businesses, it has also focused on "inter-cooperation, grassroots management, corporate social responsibility, democratic organization, and social transformation."[122] While some cooperatives, like Mondragon, have developed into large global businesses, most continue to maintain deep local connections, which protects them from the temptations of economic globalism.

Local businesses, both large and small, can offset some of the risks of global industrialization.[123] The current global economic system has largely attempted to replace family and communal businesses, which historically employed people locally. Without those local businesses, the global economic system has more easily exploited vulnerable local people. A consumer is unlikely to know how a company treats its employees when the employees are not local.[124] Therefore, maintaining a local business, like those started by GIAC, minimizes the risk of worker exploitation and environmental degradation. Local businesses illustrate how economic enterprises can succeed without going global. They demonstrate that economic enterprises can flourish without extracting the resources and labor of people outside the local market for the benefit of the people in the local market.

When churches incubate economic enterprises, they cultivate economic opportunities. Typically, churches do not have the resources to make heavy capital investments or to engineer resource extraction. Rather, they must pursue what sociologist Lewis Mumford has called an "agricultural" approach to producing something new.[125] Instead of engaging in businesses based on resource extraction, which Mumford characterizes as "mining," churches need to slowly work with their resources to grow something new.[126] By engaging in an economic process that enriches the community without unduly harming the earth or other people, churches honor God's creation and live into the *missio Dei*.

In addition to honoring the earth, this approach respects the dignity of every human being. Recall that Bauman argues that the current economic system considers many people to be "waste."[127] They are simply fodder for the economic engines. For Christians, it is important to remember that Jesus's ministry was primarily focused on the outsider and the "other." He preferred tax collectors and prostitutes over temple authorities and Roman rulers. He recognized the human dignity of individuals that the world regarded as "waste." Similarly, a cooperative approach to business development recognizes the dignity of every human being. This approach allows all people to be full-fledged and equal members of the economic community.

In listening to people who have started businesses with GIAC, it is clear that the new business owners have a profound sense of dignity and worth from their work.[128] They have created jobs for others and for themselves, and they have modeled entrepreneurship for others in their community. They exhibit pride in their accomplishments, and they are excited to share their stories. GIA has started a trend that is rippling through the community as more people begin to see the ways in which they might start a business. More important, it has shown people new ways of exercising their personal agency. As a result, the neighborhood has developed new parks, new murals, and taken a much more active role in local politics.

Using their resources and relationships, churches can help new economic enterprises and cooperatives secure the resources and develop the relationships that they need to succeed. GIAC has provided extensive training and infrastructure support for its cooperatives and their members. Notably, some of the cooperatives founded at GIAC have already started to provide training, on their own, for other entrepreneurs.[129] Cooperative businesses, like those GIAC has aided, are based on sharing responsibilities within an economic enterprise, including staffing, budgeting, and decision-making. Therefore, the new cooperative owners and operators are not alone and isolated. Rather, their cooperative projects build community, while building an economic enterprise. More important, these cooperatives have reinforced the connections within the community, and strengthened the community so that the neighborhood is now pursuing opportunities and addressing challenges that it had not considered in the past.

When churches help people start economic enterprises, they can aid economically disadvantaged communities to claim their economic power. GIAC has largely worked with members of the Latino community in Detroit.[130] The cooperatives that GIAC has partnered with have sought to overcome the economic and political disempowerment that has marked the colonial history of the last few centuries. By giving individuals the ability to create economic enterprises on their own terms and in their own ways, churches are also bringing economic life back to neighborhoods that have suffered years of neglect. They illustrate the value and talent embedded in poorly resourced communities. They can counteract chronic unemployment and understandable resentment. Last, these new enterprises, in particular cooperative businesses, can build trust in communities.[131]

While helping to start a few cooperatives will not be sufficient to overcome the damage of colonialism and the exploitation of the global economic system, it is something new and constructive that churches and communities can do to live more fully into the gospel-based values of Christianity and the *missio Dei*. They represent a constructive critique of the limitations of the current economic system. They demonstrate that there are alternatives to the status quo. This approach still risks repeating authoritarian and hierarchical pitfalls, even while it gives voice and opportunities to those who have historically been outside mainstream economic activity and suffered exploitation by those who employed them.[132] As such cooperatives grow, there is a risk that the management will start to mistreat and abuse workers and the environment in the same way as other economic players. While cooperatives have historically provided better protections for workers, they have been exploitative of the environment. Therefore, while this approach has great potential, it still requires careful oversight and a constant focus on how it serves the *missio Dei*. Going forward, GIA may need to offer more ethical formation about managing businesses, so that these businesses do not reinforce the status quo. The initial signs are very encouraging, but it will be important for the church and the community to remain diligent, and to question business leaders when their practices seem to contradict the *missio Dei*.

GIA demonstrates that a church can deploy its resources to help people leverage their labor and talent to develop their own economic enterprises. Fundamentally, GIA and GIAC are not directing these businesses; they are aiding them and learning with them. Because GIA and GIAC do not assume a dominant position, there is a much stronger possibility that the people who start these businesses can make their own decisions. As business owners and operators, these people can start to decode and deconstruct the sex-gender and race codes that have been used as social organizing practices to establish and maintain colonialism and unjust economic structures.[133] For example, the new leaders of the GIAC collectives are young Latinos, who are now serving as role models in a community where young Latinos have rarely assumed visible leadership positions. Many of GIAC's cooperatives are also led by women, which helps to confront gender biases that limited women to being employees, and not business owners and operators. Economic enterprises are central to North American culture. Therefore, when nondominant groups assume leadership roles in economic enterprises, they are debunking stereotypes and prejudices that have perpetuated oppression and marginalization for nondominant groups. Moreover, deconstructing sex-gender or race codes benefits people outside of that sex-gender group or racial group. The advances that Latinos are making at GIAC are equally beneficial for African Americans and other marginalized people.

These new business owners and operators need to realize that material security will never fully eliminate their fear and uncertainty, and paradoxically, may increase it. These new business cooperatives cannot remove the suffering and pain that exists in the world, but they may provide momentary relief to global fear, and they may even offer hope.[134] The new business owners, who were once the "other," must also resist the systemic push for them to "other" another. These same sex-gender and racial codes that held the new business owners back will continue to seek to hold others back, so that there is still labor that can be exploited to fuel the current economic system. The new business owners and operators must be careful that they do not find themselves inflicting injustices on others, in the same way that injustices were inflicted on them.

As these new cooperatives grow, there will be multiple forces that will want to co-opt these businesses because they tell hopeful stories and suggest a redemptive pathway for capitalism. These new business owners will also need to be on guard against co-opting other people's stories to advance their own stories or businesses. To the extent that these new businesses are cooperative and collaborative business enterprises, competitors may look to prey upon them as well.[135] Therefore, GIA can offer guidance, education, and formation so that the new cooperatives do not inadvertently become part of the economic status quo. By committing to livable wages, health benefits, and profit sharing, these cooperatives can demonstrate an alternative form of economic enterprise.

Once these new church-based economic enterprises have been established, the church has no long-term oversight of the operations. For example, GIA has no control over the cooperatives sponsored by GIAC. Churches may not be able to prevent businesses that they help launch from exploiting others. Churches may try to provide oversight and regulations, but such an approach risks perpetuating the past oppressive roles of Christian churches. If a church does not continue to own an economic enterprise that it helped to start, then it can only provide moral leadership and guidance. Churches must be willing to freely share in the creation of these businesses and then step away from them.

Theologian and Pastor Gil Rendle argues that local congregations are uniquely positioned to redirect North American culture back towards communalism, akin to Ibn Khaldun's concept of *asabiyya*. Rendle notes that, historically, North America has oscillated between an obsession with individualism and a commitment to community.[136] Rendle cautions that the renewed communal focus cannot rest upon scapegoating marginalized groups, as it has in the past. Xenophobia and other forms of exclusion are not a sustainable way of renewing community. They may create some short-term alliances, but they will not provide long-term renewals. State and economic institutions have thrived under the reign of individualism, and they have reinforced it. By contrast, local congregations are equipped to pay attention to individuals, while helping to bring them together into a community. Local congregations exist in neighborhoods where it is possible to build personal relationships and trust, just like GIA in Detroit. With those relationships in place, local congregations can facilitate compromise and collaboration.[137] They also encourage community members to work together, without the church. GIA's Detroit neighborhood has witnessed strong neighborhood renewal because of the collaboration occurring in the community. GIA has helped to foster that collaboration, which could be its greatest expression of the *missio Dei*. It has contributed to the reconciliation of the neighbors to each other and to God's creation.

Rendle posits that churches should become platforms for community organizing.[138] They can offer their facilities to members of the community, regardless of whether they are church members. GIA relied upon community organizing to launch its church, and ultimately, it relied upon community organizing to incubate the cooperatives too. GIA has applied community organizing to church planting and to local economic development. GIA does not set the agenda or the time frame for these new community activities, but it supports and fosters them in any way possible.[139] In other words, GIA is sharing its power. It is modeling the radical hospitality that marked Jesus's ministry, as well as sharing resources that marked the early Christian communities. Moreover, it has inspired others in the community to do the same, which is resulting in numerous benefits for the whole neighborhood.

Admittedly, most clergy are not interested in or trained for helping people start businesses. Therefore, asking them to do so might be intimidating. When they started GIA, John Cummins and Meghan Sobocienski certainly found themselves in unfamiliar territory, and they admit to being initially overwhelmed.[140] Like John and Meghan, most clergy would find themselves in a type of borderland, navigating between church and business. They may feel humbled, like the "other," in doing this work, because they do not understand the business world around them. Nevertheless, clergy may be the strongest ally for their neighbors. As a result, clergy may have to venture into these unfamiliar borderlands. They may, in fact, be uniquely qualified to help community members navigate the borders between being a business owner and a customer, being an employer and an employee, and being employed and unemployed.

Some members of a congregation may object to the clergy person helping someone to start a business. It might seem like a transgression, a blurring of the bright line between church and business, sacred and secular. In John and Meghan's case, their congregants did not object. They started the GIAC soon after founding GIA. In some cases, however, the situation could be more challenging. The clergy might be helping to start a business that will compete with an existing business in the community. Starting businesses can be sensitive. Therefore, the process requires considerable discernment, transparency, and communication, which can minimize potential conflict.

Grace in Action Church demonstrates that Christian congregations can pursue their mission in new ways. By working with historically marginalized people, churches can develop alternatives to the current economic system. Churches can promote new forms of economic enterprises that move beyond some of the exploitative colonial economic practices of the past. They can provide examples of "shareholding/postindustrial capitalism," and embrace Ibn Khaldun's concept of *asabiyya*. Economic enterprises can provide new life for their congregations, their communities, and most important, the people in their communities, who are, regardless of their faith tradition, the people of God. GIA and GIAC illustrate several principles that have been consistent in the prior case studies, and that demonstrate the ways that congregations can simultaneously engage in missional renewal, social justice, and economic sustainability.

1. **The primary focus must be missional, not financial.** John Cummins and Meghan Sobocienski went to Detroit to plant a Lutheran church, not to start cooperatives.[141] They were funded by the synod, and they faced an uncertain financial future. But John and Meghan used their community organizing backgrounds to understand the needs of their neighborhood, and they discovered that their mission included starting business cooperatives.
2. **A clergy person does not need a business background or entrepreneurial experience to start new businesses.** Rather, they need to be willing to conduct an honest asset assessment of the congregation. John and Meghan had worked in the Lutheran church, and they had experience with community organizing, but they had never started a cooperative or a business. Nevertheless, they were willing to try to help the people in their midst. They recognized that their mission was taking them into an unfamiliar field.
3. **Leaders need to be committed for the long term.** Meghan and John have ten years of ministry at GIA and GIAC, and they have already demonstrated a deep commitment to their mission and to their neighborhood. Transforming a

missional and economic model takes patience and time, and Meghan and John are offering both. In addition, the people who have started cooperatives have demonstrated a long-term commitment to helping other people start cooperatives, too.

4. **Leaders must be willing to experiment with new models of mission, including new financial models.** GIA and GIAC have started a series of cooperatives and have developed a number of secular partnerships to advance their mission. Their ministry looks different than traditional Lutheran ministries, but it is responding to the needs of God's people. As a result, it embodies the *missio Dei*.
5. **Active lay leadership is essential.** Meghan and John have not developed these cooperatives on their own; they are emanating from the community. They are empowering community leaders to start these cooperatives, and now, many of those leaders are helping others to start businesses, as well as other community initiatives.
6. **Mission emerges from supporting people on the margins.** GIA and GIAC provide support for people who have historically been economically oppressed by the current economic systems. They are helping these people to reclaim their power, particularly their economic power. With a new sense of their own agency, people in GIA's neighborhood are orchestrating a revitalization of their entire community.
7. **Congregations must know their local ecosystem.** GIA and GIAC know the local ecosystem. Meghan and John conducted hours of interviews before they started their ministry, and they remain very active in the local community. They live there. They have remodeled buildings in the neighborhood. They are a vital part of their community.
8. **Faith and mission must be at the center.** Faith and missional commitment undergird all GIA and GIAC work.

> Their ministries and the cooperatives evidence the constant and creative power of God. Moreover, the work demonstrates that there are alternatives to the current economic system, and that local church-founded cooperatives can make a difference in people's lives. Finally, they demonstrate that there are ways to offer renewed agency to individuals and communities so that they can fully live into God's hope for them.

PROVIDING CRUCIAL SERVICES: ST. PETER'S EPISCOPAL CHURCH, DARTMOUTH, MASSACHUSETTS

St. Peter's Episcopal Church (SPE) is an Episcopal church in the small town of Dartmouth (pop. 33,783), which is located in southeastern Massachusetts, just north of the Rhode Island border.[142] Unlike the other case studies in this book, SPE's ministry is not in an urban context, but a rural and suburban context. Dartmouth is part of Bristol County, Massachusetts (pop. 579,200), and it is part of the Providence-Warwick, RI-MA Metropolitan Statistical Area.[143] Dartmouth is adjacent to the Massachusetts city of Fall River (pop. 93,840).[144] It also sits on the south coast of Massachusetts, which has historically been agricultural land. It abuts Buzzards Bay and provides easy access to several coastal islands, which has increasingly made Dartmouth a vacation destination. Finally, Dartmouth is home to the University of Massachusetts, Dartmouth campus, which currently has 7,759 students and 3,82 full-time faculty.[145] It is the smallest of the University of Massachusetts campuses.

Unlike the other case studies in this book, SPE does not minister to a BIPOC community, but to a largely white congregation. Within its congregation, SPE has been particularly welcoming to the LGBTQI+ community, and it has been very attentive to people with mental health needs. Like many rural and suburban congregations, SPE was facing rapidly declining membership. The Episcopal Diocese of Massachusetts was seriously considering closing the congregation.

However, the Rev. Scott A. Ciosek was able to convince the diocesan staff to give him a little time to work on a renewal project.[146] The diocese has provided substantial resources over the years to aid SPE's transition.

SPE serves the town of Dartmouth, which encompasses Bristol County Census tract 6532 and Bristol County Census tract 6533. These areas are far wealthier than the other census tracts described in this book. In tract 6532, 6.5% of the population lives below the poverty line, and in tract 6533, 7.3% of the population lives below the poverty line. Both tracts have far lower levels of poverty than the national average, which is 13% of the census track living in poverty. The median income is $131,733 for tract 6532, and $108,500 for tract 6533, compared to the median national income of $69,000.[147] In tract 6532, 53.5% of the renters pay over 30% of their household income in rent, while that percentage is 42.8% in tract 6533. In tract 6532, 1.1% of the population does not have health insurance, while that percentage is 0.3% in tract 6533. Nationally, 9% of the population does not have health insurance. In tract 6532, 13.8% of the population does not have access to the internet, while the percentage is 10.4% in tract 6533. Both fall short of the national average of just 10% of the population without internet access.[148] Despite having more resources in its community than the other churches in this book, SPE faced the same challenges as those other churches when addressing missional renewal, congregational growth, and financial viability.

SPE was founded in 1956. Initially, the congregation moved into the former St. Mary's Catholic Church on Elm Street in Dartmouth.[149] As the congregation grew, St. Peter's purchased its first parish house in 1959. This building remains on St. Peter's campus, and it currently houses offices, meeting spaces, and classrooms. In June 1963, SPE broke ground for a new church. It was originally built as a temporary structure. It was formally dedicated in April 1963. Throughout much of this time, St. Peter's offered a vibrant ministry to Dartmouth, Fall River, and the surrounding community. However, like so many other churches, SPE faced major declines in the early twenty-first century. By 2013, its average Sunday attendance (ASA) had dropped to eighteen.

Rev. Ciosek came to SPE in 2013; for the prior seven years he had worked in hospice, grief, and supportive services. Prior to his hospice work, he had been a Roman Catholic priest in the Fall River area.[150] When he arrived at SPE, the congregation had an average Sunday attendance (ASA) of six, and on some Sundays, there were as many as ten attendees. The congregation was elderly and insular.[151] Generally, the congregation was happy to gather for an hour on Sunday and then close up the church for the remainder of the week.

Within a year of serving at SPE, Ciosek saw the need for counseling resources in Dartmouth and the South Coast of Massachusetts. In 2014, the South Coast was heavily impacted by the opioid epidemic, and there were very few mental health resources. In fact, even today, there are still limited mental health resources on the South Coast. It can take six to eight months just to secure an initial mental health intake appointment.[152] In addition, SPE had a large house located on its campus called the Bridge House. When Ciosek arrived at SPE, it was largely used for storage. In 2014, the SPE vestry was discussing how to rent part of the Bridge House. After a lengthy vestry meeting, Ciosek recounts going into the SPE parking lot late the same evening, looking up to the sky, and feeling a deep call to use the Bridge House for ministry to serve the surrounding community.[153] He felt compelled to answer the question, How can this property reach everyone in this community?[154] He started to discern about how the property could do the work of Jesus and how it could offer hope and healing to the Dartmouth community.[155] He started to consider ways that SPE could do more than just collect rent from tenants in The Bridge House; he started to really pray about how SPE could offer transformative ministry and missional renewal there. He looked for the *missio Dei* for that location.

After prayerful discernment and a careful analysis of the community assets and needs, Ciosek developed The Bridge: A Center for Hope and Healing, which is a 501 (c)(3) nonprofit organization, located in the Bridge House. The Bridge has developed into a vibrant counseling and support program, and it addresses the tremendous need for mental health support in the surrounding rural communities. The Bridge accepts all major health insurance providers and offers cash payment options for those people who are not covered by health insurance. Ciosek serves as the executive director of The Bridge, which employed five licensed psychotherapists, as well as an intake coordinator and a financial administrator, as of April 2025.[156] The Bridge is experiencing tremendous growth.[157] As a result, it is considering hiring its first full-time clinical director and opening a satellite location with another Episcopal church in the Diocese of Massachusetts.

With the success of The Bridge, SPE has seen several signs of missional renewal and congregational growth. Ciosek points out that while many people first arrive on the campus at SPE for The Bridge, many ultimately find their way into the church. The Bridge does not do any proselytizing or evangelizing for SPE, but it demonstrates SPE's commitment to hope and healing. It provides a manifestation of the community's mission and its commitment to gospel values. In addition, it demonstrates that SPE is a safe place for all people, particularly the LGBTQI+ community. The members of the LGBTQI+ community in Dartmouth who were interviewed for this book are grateful for SPE. They feel like they have a home, and a place where they are fully accepted. As a result, many people in the LGBTQI+ community have become much more involved in SPE and in the larger community. With a sense of safety, they have also developed a stronger sense of their personal agency. In the parking lot on SPE's campus, there is a large sign that reads, "Come Find the Peace Within," and it lists the Sunday service time. Remarkably, many people heed the sign's advice, and they come to SPE to worship. With their renewed sense of peace and dignity, they are going back out into the community and bringing the *missio Dei* to life.

Ultimately, The Bridge provided SPE with a new missional focus, which led to a new financial model, as well as dramatic congregational growth. While the pandemic curtailed attendance, SPE had an ASA of over 56 prior to the pandemic, well above its low of 18 in 2013 and 21 in 2014. In 2022 and 2021, SPE had an ASA of 47 and 46, respectively, as seen in figure 2.6, which is well in line with ASA

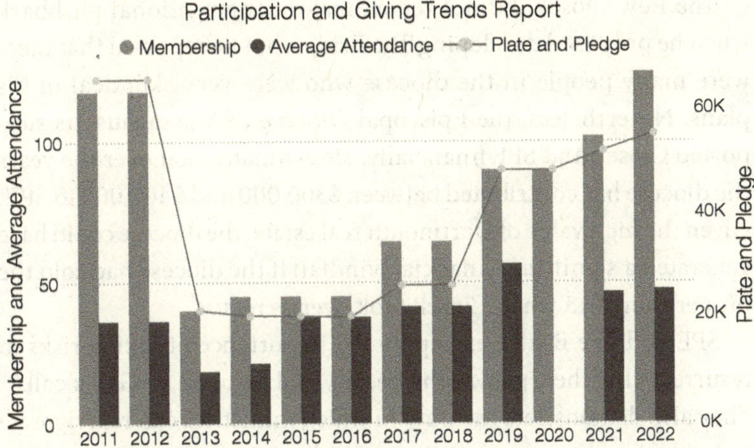

Figure 2.6. St. Peter's Episcopal Membership, Attendance, and Giving Trends.[159]
Source: Episcopal Church Research and Statistics.

across the Episcopal Diocese of Massachusetts. Since the pandemic, membership has not reached prior levels, but ASA is still well above levels a decade ago, which is not true for the majority of Episcopal churches. In addition, SPE continues to attract young people and young families. As a result, SPE recently added a new curate, Rev. Faith Mbuthia, to its staff as its new Director of Youth and Family Ministry. Rev. Ciosek received a three-year grant of $150,000 to hire an assistant lay chaplain to join him in his work as the Episcopal campus minister at the University of Massachusetts's Dartmouth campus.

The Rev. Ciosek is a dynamic leader, but it is more than strong preaching that is drawing people to SPE. People see how active SPE and The Bridge are in the community. Because of all its community outreach and programming, hundreds of people come to SPE every week.[158] Some come for counseling, others are looking for a safe space for LGBTQI+ folks, and others are looking for a community that is truly welcoming and inclusive. SPE's work in the community vividly illustrates their commitment to the gospel and to the *missio Dei.* Their dedication to mission has driven congregational growth and financial security.

The Rev. Ciosek did not report major congregational pushback when he proposed developing The Bridge, but he reported that there were many people in the diocese who were very skeptical of his plans. Nevertheless, the Episcopal Diocese of Massachusetts supported Ciosek and SPE financially. He estimates that over the years the diocese has contributed between $300,000 and $400,000 to SPE. Given the high value of Dartmouth real estate, the diocese could have generated a significant financial windfall if the diocese had sold the property in 2013 when Ciosek took over as rector.

SPE and The Bridge exemplify the importance of taking risks to resurrect churches, preach the gospel, and respond to God's call.[160] They also demonstrate the ways in which ministries can reinvigorate individual and communal agency. With a renewed sense of agency, individuals and communities can have an enormous impact. The other case studies in this book have reinforced the importance of empowering historically marginalized people as one way to start to dismantle unjust economic systems of oppression.[161] SPE has largely served a white community, but it has also served historically marginalized groups. It has supported the LGBTQI+ community, which has been marginalized in the region. SPE serves a rural community, and rural communities have also been marginalized and overlooked by many of the dominant economic forces, as well as the Episcopal Church.

Some critics worry that replicating SPE's mission requires clergy to have business experience. The Rev. Ciosek points out that he knew nothing about starting a counseling center. He had worked in hospices and grief counseling prior to SPE, but he had no entrepreneurial experience.[162] The Rev. Ciosek does not receive 100 percent of his compensation from the church. SPE covers just 25 percent of his salary. Ciosek supplements his priest income with his income for serving as the executive director of The Bridge, and for serving as the campus chaplain at the University of Massachusetts Dartmouth. SPE and Ciosek prevent confusion between the roles by providing very clear expectations and definitions for his various roles. However, just like the other cases, SPE and The Bridge demonstrate the viability of this approach. SPE is the beneficiary of Ciosek working on the SPE campus full time. SPE and Ciosek have set very clear boundaries and expectations because of his dual role at SPE and The Bridge. Ciosek routinely reminds the vestry and congregation that he is only paid by SPE for one quarter of his time. Nevertheless, SPE is thriving because of Ciosek's 100% commitment to ministry and mission in his Dartmouth location. As more churches follow SPE's example, it will be increasingly important to become clear about overlapping roles and responsibilities. With care and discernment, it is possible to develop a clear consensus on expectations, just like SPE and The Bridge.

Like so many of the other clergy leaders described in this book, Rev. Ciosek is not a lifelong Episcopalian. He was ordained as a priest in the Roman Catholic Church, and he came to SPE after he was received into the Episcopal Church from the Roman Catholic Church. At first, Ciosek faced resistance from some existing congregants. Not everyone was pleased with the new focus on mission, rather than exclusively prioritizing traditional Episcopal worship. But he withstood the resistance because the leadership team had carefully discerned about the changes that were necessary for SPE to continue in ministry. SPE did not reach complete consensus about The Bridge. Leaders need boldness and conviction.

SPE demonstrates several critical features for churches considering alternative missional and financial models:

1. **The primary focus must be missional, not financial.** SPE saw the need for more counseling resources in their community. The congregation understood how ministry could provide hope and healing, and SPE understood how hope and healing fit within the *missio Dei*. SPE and The Bridge prove that there are ways that a missional focus can generate the resources necessary to operate church ministries.
2. **A clergy person does not need a business background or entrepreneurial experience to start new businesses.** Rather, a clergy leader needs to be willing to conduct an honest asset assessment of the congregation and the needs

of the community. Rev. Ciosek has the most essential entrepreneurial quality; he is willing to try something new.

3. **Leaders need to be committed for the long term.** Rev. Ciosek has been serving SPE for several years, and he has spent much of that time also leading The Bridge as its executive director. Moreover, he envisions staying at SPE for the remainder of his career, which is almost another twenty years. Transforming a missional and economic model takes patience and time. As a result, it is also critical that clergy have the support and self-care necessary to sustain themselves in these roles.
4. **All leaders need to be willing to experiment with new models of mission, as well as new models of church finance.** At SPE, Ciosek is not intimidated by experimentation or afraid of failure. He has realistic expectations, and he is willing to discontinue a program or policy if it is not working for the community.
5. **Active lay leadership is essential.** The Rev. Ciosek did not rely as heavily upon lay leaders as those in the other case studies, but he still looks to lay leaders to help guide SPE and The Bridge.
6. **Mission emerges from supporting people on the margins.** SPE provides support for people who have little to no sources for mental health and spiritual support. Their challenges might have been overlooked or ignored if SPE had not committed to the missional work of mental health.
7. **Congregations must know their local ecosystem.** SPE knows its local ecosystem, and it actively partners with all sorts of individuals and organizations. SPE and The Bridge know the local university, the community organizations, the private foundations, and the government agencies.[163] Similarly, before starting on any new venture, it is critical that a church knows its local ecosystem very well.
8. **Faith and mission must be at the center.** In all SPE's work, spirituality and mission play a key role. The Rev. Ciosek

takes his vocation to the priesthood seriously, and his congregation is deeply committed to the sacraments and the baptismal covenant. Even more so than in other case studies, Ciosek's call to start The Bridge was the result of a divine encounter and deep spiritual reflection. People attend Sunday services because of the missional work that SPE and The Bridge are doing the rest of the week. By leading with missional work, a healthy financial model has followed. A financial challenge does not need to be a reason for despair; it can be an opportunity for new mission. It can lead more fully to the *missio Dei.*

CHAPTER 3

Quantitative Data

The case studies in chapter 2 demonstrate how and why a church might launch an economic venture, but they do not prove that a church-based enterprise will actually renew mission and grow congregations just because they did in these cases. To demonstrate a correlation between church-based economic enterprises and missional growth and congregational growth, I conducted surveys of individuals and clergy whose churches generate at least 15% of revenue from economic enterprises. The surveys were conducted through SurveyMonkey, which is an online survey tool. As part of its service, SurveyMonkey can curate panels of respondents that would be most appropriate to one's research objective. In these surveys, I requested panels of people that self-identified as Christian, Roman Catholic, or Protestant. There was no way of confirming their identities. However, in the second and third surveys, I asked for the name and location of their congregation, which helped me to cross-check those communities and their ministries.

When initiating the first survey, it was unclear that there would be a material number of churches that generated 15% of revenue from economic enterprises. Therefore, the survey started with over 350 respondents to find 251 whose churches had economic enterprises and 224 whose churches had economic enterprises that contributed over 15% of revenue. The first survey did not ask about the types of economic enterprises because it was unclear whether there would be a statistically significant number of respondents. The second survey asked additional questions about the types of economic enterprises and the demographics of the congregations. The second survey also revisited the same questions as the first survey, to verify the results of the first survey. The first two surveys were conducted with members of churches that started economic enterprises, rather than the clergy or church leadership. Therefore, to test the accuracy of results, a third survey was completed of 64 clergy who were part of churches that had developed economic enterprises that contributed at least 15% of their churches' revenue.

With SurveyMonkey, there is no way to follow-up with survey respondents or to confirm their identity, which are major drawbacks and limit the reliability of the SurveyMonkey data. Ideally, when conducting a survey, one would be able to follow-up with survey respondents at a later date to verify the ongoing accuracy of the information.[1] Fortunately, SurveyMonkey can provide a statistically significant number of responses, which were very helpful in this research project. SurveyMonkey responses alone might not be sufficient for solid practical theology research, but SurveyMonkey was helpful when combined with other methodologies, like the case studies and focus groups used in this project. In addition, SurveyMonkey assures the anonymity and privacy of the survey respondents. Despite some drawbacks, these surveys provided some valuable insights. Based on these three surveys, church members and clergy certainly believe that church-based economic enterprises drive both mission and membership.

The first survey was conducted on July 13, 2024, through SurveyMonkey. As shown in figures 3.1 and 3.3, the survey found that 90% of the 224 respondents saw an increase in mission and membership after their church started an economic enterprise.

As seen in figure 3.2, of the 203 respondents who reported missional growth, 59% reported greater community engagement, 55% reported more outreach, 54% reported increased educational programming, 45% reported more member involvement, and 29% reported more volunteerism. Even among the 22 respondents that

Q5 Have you experienced a renewal of mission since your church opened the economic enterprise?

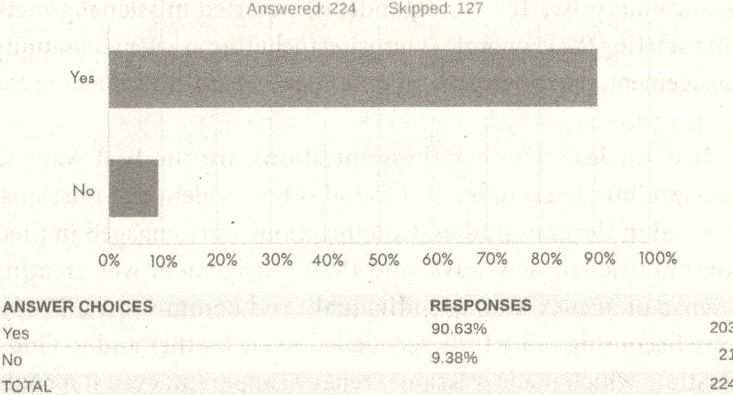

ANSWER CHOICES	RESPONSES	
Yes	90.63%	203
No	9.38%	21
TOTAL		224

Figure 3.1. Survey #1, Question 5: Missional Increase
Source: Church-Based Economic Enterprises Survey, July 13, 2024, n=351.

Q6 How has the missional renewal manifested at your church?

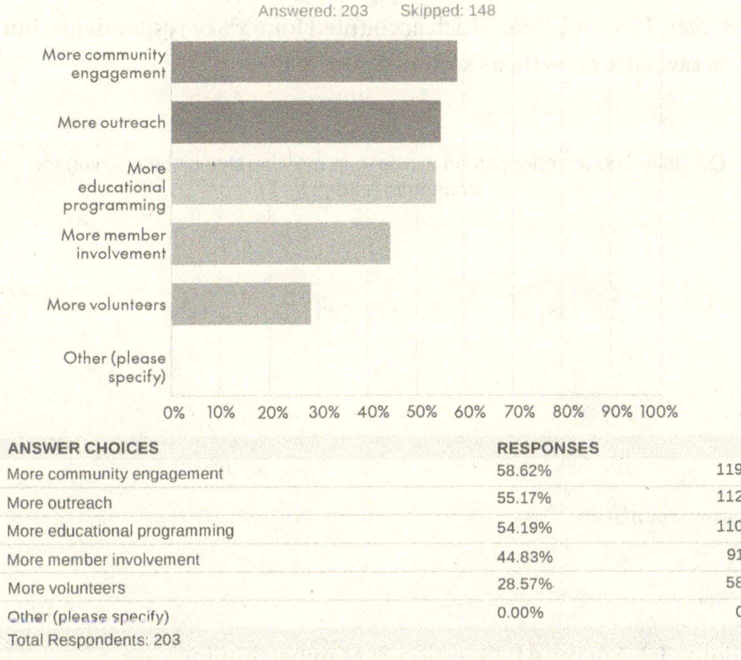

ANSWER CHOICES	RESPONSES	
More community engagement	58.62%	119
More outreach	55.17%	112
More educational programming	54.19%	110
More member involvement	44.83%	91
More volunteers	28.57%	58
Other (please specify)	0.00%	0
Total Respondents: 203		

Figure 3.2. Survey #1, Question 6: Types of Missional Increase.
Source: Church-Based Economic Enterprises Survey, July 13, 2024, n=351.

did not experience an increase in membership after starting an economic enterprise, 41% (9 respondents) reported missional growth after starting the economic enterprise, including greater community engagement, more outreach, and more member involvement in the congregation.

It is unclear whether these questions are the best ways to measure missional renewal. I found other evidence of missional renewal in the case studies. Congregations were engaged in their communities in new ways, and their engagement was creating a sense of agency among individuals and communities. People were becoming more fully reconciled to each other and to God's creation, which made missional renewal apparent, even if it could not be quantified.

As seen in figure 3.3, the survey found the membership growth also increased by 90%.

In those that saw membership growth, the growth was generally between 10% and 15%, which accounted for 63% of respondents, but 17% saw 20% growth, as seen in figure 3.4.

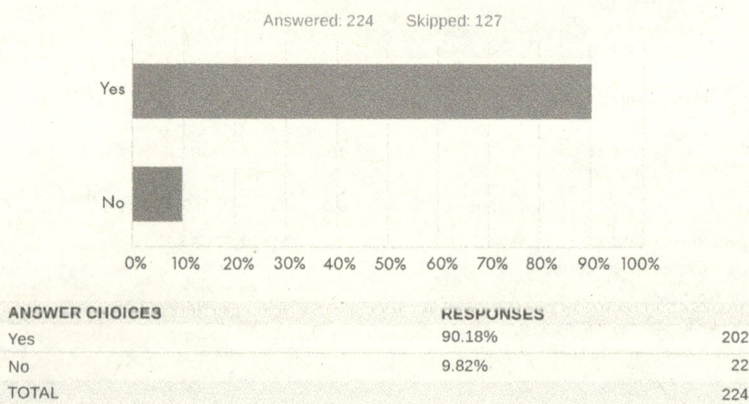

ANSWER CHOICES	RESPONSES	
Yes	90.18%	202
No	9.82%	22
TOTAL		224

Figure 3.3. Survey #1, Question 3: Membership Increase.
Source: Church-Based Economic Enterprises Survey, July 13, 2024, n=351.

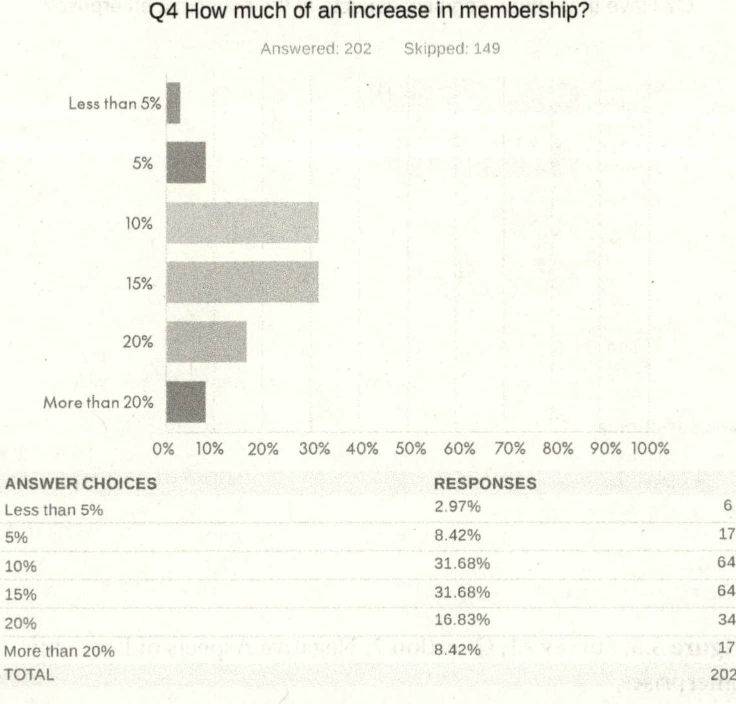

ANSWER CHOICES	RESPONSES	
Less than 5%	2.97%	6
5%	8.42%	17
10%	31.68%	64
15%	31.68%	64
20%	16.83%	34
More than 20%	8.42%	17
TOTAL		202

Figure 3.4. Survey #1, Question 4: Amount of Increase.
Source: Church-Based Economic Enterprises Survey, July 13, 2024, n=351.

The survey also found that the economic enterprises are not universally positive, as evident in figure 3.5. While they may drive missional renewal, congregational growth, and financial sustainability, they also distract clergy, confuse the congregation, and take away from what is currently perceived as "mission." Only 25% of the 224 respondents said that the economic enterprise had no negative aspects. Of the 224 respondents, 45% said that the economic enterprise distracted the clergy, and 41% said that it confused the congregation. In these cases, people are perceiving traditional Sunday worship as the primary responsibility of clergy and the congregation. Additional formation might help to expand their understanding of mission. Therefore, clear boundaries, guidelines, and communications are necessary for congregations to most successfully develop

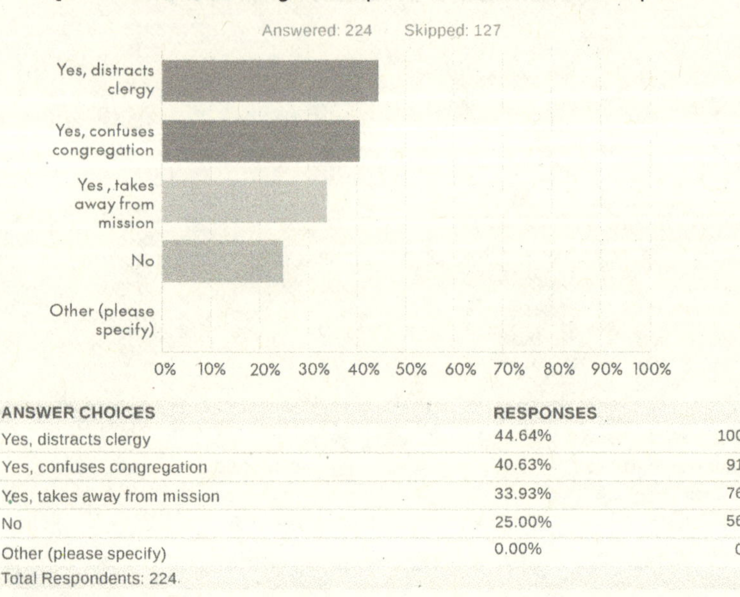

ANSWER CHOICES	RESPONSES	
Yes, distracts clergy	44.64%	100
Yes, confuses congregation	40.63%	91
Yes, takes away from mission	33.93%	76
No	25.00%	56
Other (please specify)	0.00%	0
Total Respondents: 224		

Figure 3.5. Survey #1, Question 7: Negative Aspects of Economic Enterprises.
Source: Church-Based Economic Enterprises Survey, July 13, 2024, n=351.

economic enterprises. In the case studies above, the churches and their leaders established clear boundaries and consistent communication to minimize the challenges identified in the survey. They also constantly reiterated the ways in which these new economic ministries reinforced the *missio Dei*.

Despite the negative aspects of church-based economic enterprises, the first survey's demonstration of the overwhelmingly positive impact on missional renewal and congregational growth provides ample evidence for congregations to discern about starting an economic enterprise.

The second survey was conducted on August 31, 2024, also through SurveyMonkey. The survey started with over 505 respondents to find 321 whose churches had economic enterprises, and 261 whose churches had economic enterprises that contributed over 15% of revenue. In addition, the second survey asked about the details of the churches' economic enterprises and the demographics of the congregations.

As seen in figure 3.6, the second survey found that 79% of the 261 respondents reported an increase in mission. The results of the second survey were slightly lower than the 90% reported in the first survey, but still surprisingly strong.

As illustrated in figure 3.7, of the 207 respondents to this follow-up question, 51% reported greater community engagement, 66% reported more outreach, 42% reported increased educational programming, 40% reported more member involvement, and 30% reported more volunteerism. Churches with for-profit economic enterprises experienced more missional growth than those with nonprofits. Of the 78 churches with for-profit enterprises, 86% reported missional growth after starting the enterprise, including 64% that reported an increase in outreach after starting the economic enterprise. Even among the 59 respondents that did not experience an increase in membership, 42% (25 respondents) reported missional growth after starting the economic enterprise, including 84% (21 respondents) that reported an increase in outreach.

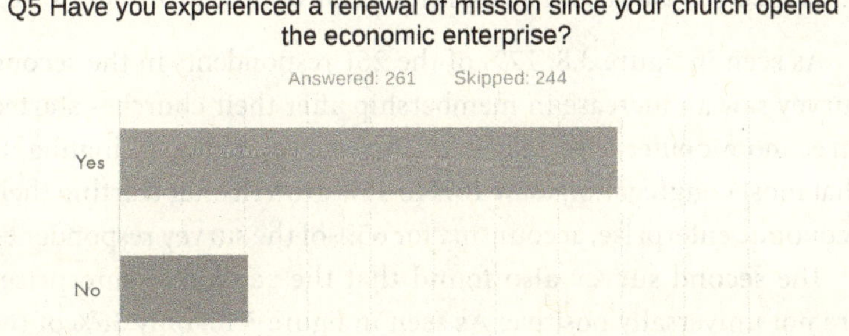

ANSWER CHOICES	RESPONSES	
Yes	79.31%	207
No	20.69%	54
TOTAL		261

Figure 3.6. Survey #2, Question 5: Missional Increase.
Source: Church-Based Economic Enterprises Survey, August 31, 2024, n=505.

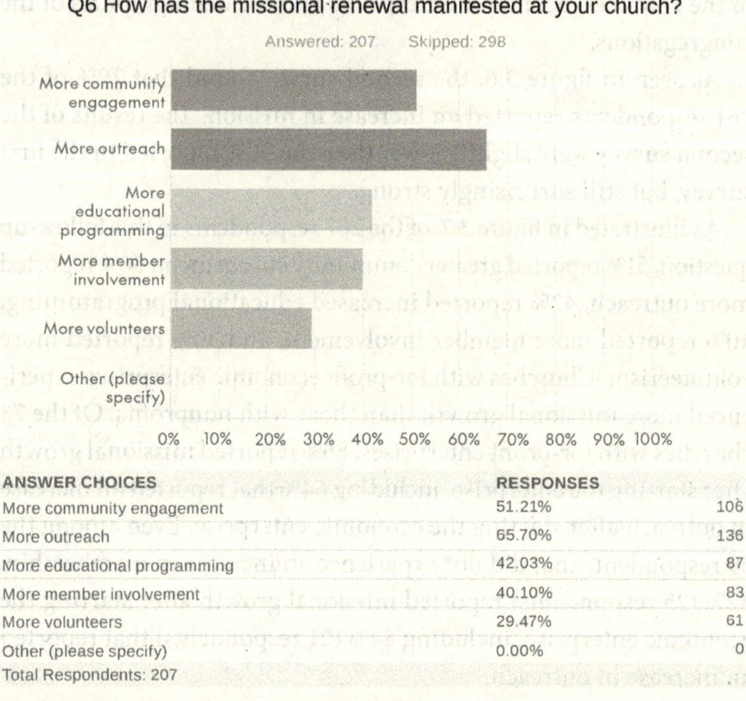

ANSWER CHOICES	RESPONSES	
More community engagement	51.21%	106
More outreach	65.70%	136
More educational programming	42.03%	87
More member involvement	40.10%	83
More volunteers	29.47%	61
Other (please specify)	0.00%	0
Total Respondents: 207		

Figure 3.7. Survey #2, Question 6: Types of Missional Increase.
Source: Church-Based Economic Enterprises Survey, August 31, 2024, n=505.

As seen in figure 3.8, 77% of the 261 respondents in the second survey saw an increase in membership after their churches started an economic enterprise. Like in the first survey, figure 3.9 highlights that most congregations saw 10% to 15% growth after starting their economic enterprise, accounting for 65% of the survey respondents.

The second survey also found that the economic enterprises are not universally positive. As seen in figure 3.10, only 36% of the 261 respondents said that the economic enterprise had no negative aspects. Of the 261 respondents, 33% said that the economic enterprise distracted the clergy and 31% said that it confused the congregation. Again, these responses reflect a limited view of the role of clergy and of the congregation. Additional formation might help people to understand that the work of economic development fits well within the *missio Dei.*

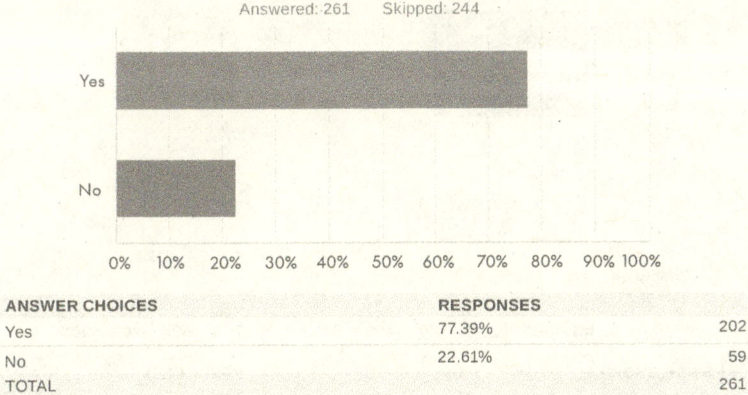

ANSWER CHOICES	RESPONSES	
Yes	77.39%	202
No	22.61%	59
TOTAL		261

Figure 3.8. Survey #2, Question 3: Membership Increase.
Source: Church-Based Economic Enterprises Survey, August 31, 2024, n=505.

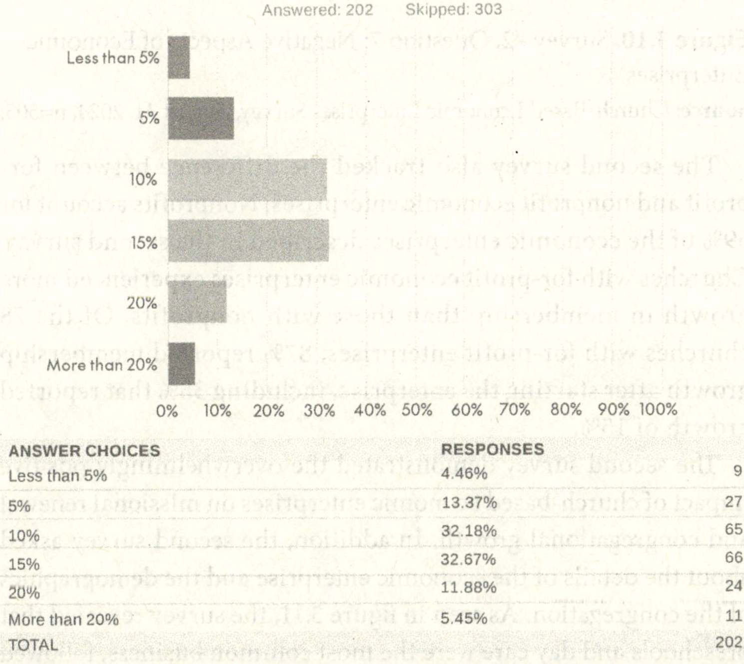

ANSWER CHOICES	RESPONSES	
Less than 5%	4.46%	9
5%	13.37%	27
10%	32.18%	65
15%	32.67%	66
20%	11.88%	24
More than 20%	5.45%	11
TOTAL		202

Figure 3.9. Survey #2, Question 4: Amount of Membership Increase.
Source: Church-Based Economic Enterprises Survey, August 31, 2024, n=505.

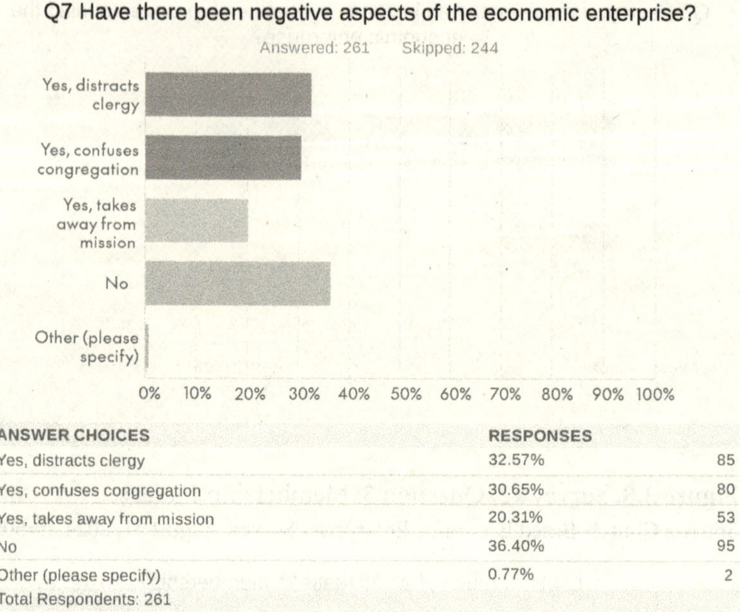

ANSWER CHOICES	RESPONSES	
Yes, distracts clergy	32.57%	85
Yes, confuses congregation	30.65%	80
Yes, takes away from mission	20.31%	53
No	36.40%	95
Other (please specify)	0.77%	2
Total Respondents: 261		

Figure 3.10. Survey #2, Question 7: Negative Aspects of Economic Enterprises.
Source: Church-Based Economic Enterprises Survey, August 31, 2024, n=505.

The second survey also tracked the difference between for-profit and nonprofit economic enterprises. Nonprofits account for 69% of the economic enterprises described in the second survey. Churches with for-profit economic enterprises experienced more growth in membership than those with nonprofits. Of the 78 churches with for-profit enterprises, 87% reported membership growth after starting the enterprise, including 38% that reported growth of 15%.

The second survey demonstrated the overwhelmingly positive impact of church-based economic enterprises on missional renewal and congregational growth. In addition, the second survey asked about the details of the economic enterprise and the demographics of the congregation. As seen in figure 3.11, the survey revealed that preschools and day care were the most common business, followed by thrift shops and then coffee shops.

Q10 How would you describe your church-based economic enterprise?

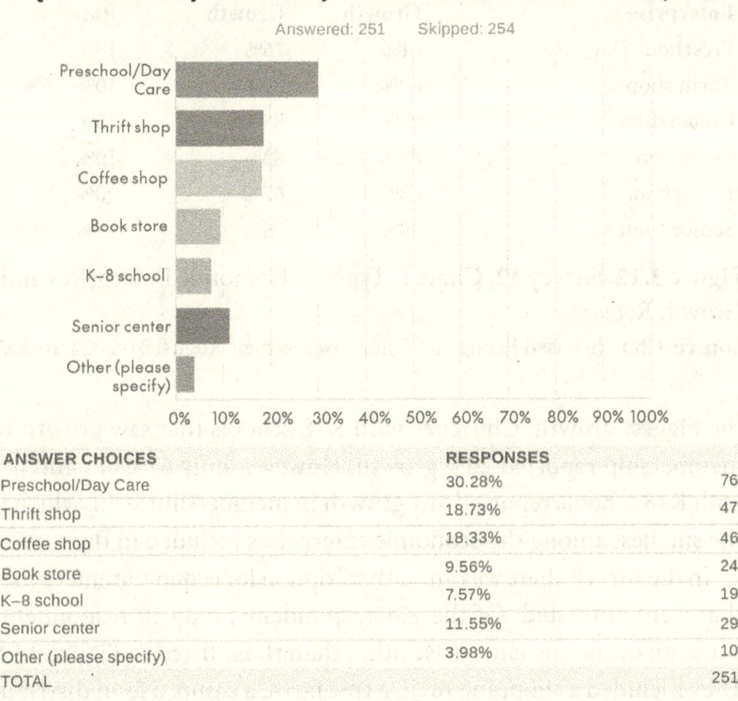

ANSWER CHOICES	RESPONSES	
Preschool/Day Care	30.28%	76
Thrift shop	18.73%	47
Coffee shop	18.33%	46
Book store	9.56%	24
K–8 school	7.57%	19
Senior center	11.55%	29
Other (please specify)	3.98%	10
TOTAL		251

Figure 3.11. Survey #2, Question 10: Describe Your Church-Based Economic Enterprise.
Source: Church-Based Economic Enterprises Survey, August 31, 2024, n=505.

In analyzing the data about the different types of economic enterprises, figure 3.12 describes the missional and congregational growth experienced from the impact of those different enterprises. In figure 3.12, the second column reports the percentage of congregations that reported missional growth. The third column reports the percentage of congregations that reported growth in membership after starting that type of economic enterprise. The fourth column lists the most frequent membership growth reported associated with that type of economic enterprise. Based on these findings, thrift shops and coffee shops are most likely to drive missional growth, while coffee shops are the most likely economic enterprise to drive membership growth. For the best overall growth in membership, K–8 schools seem to drive

Economic Enterprise	Missional Growth	Membership Growth	Growth Rate
Preschool/Day care	81%	76%	15%
Thrift shop	87%	79%	10%–15%
Coffee shop	87%	85%	15%
Book store	84%	83%	10%
K–8 school	63%	67%	20%
Senior center	79%	76%	15%

Figure 3.12. Survey #2, Chart 1: Types of Economic Enterprises and Growth Rates.
Source: Church-Based Economic Enterprises Survey, August 31, 2024, n=505.

the biggest growth. Churches with K–8 schools that saw growth in membership reported 20% growth. However, only 67% of churches with K–8 schools reported any growth in membership at all, which is the smallest among the economic enterprises included in the survey.

In the survey, there was an "Other" option for economic enterprises that were not listed. Of the 251 respondents, only 10 respondents chose an economic enterprise other than those listed in Figure 3.12. They included a shopping mall, a tree farm, a camp, a food distribution center, and a rental space. It was surprising how many churches had started one of the six economic enterprises listed in Figure 3.12. These are fairly traditional enterprises for churches, and as the survey shows, they yield great benefits in missional and membership growth.

In addition, figure 3.13 shows that churches that just collect rent also see strong growth from the economic enterprises that are started on their campuses. Of the 68 respondents that only collected rent, and not additional income, 85% saw missional growth, and 82% saw membership growth, with 15% growth as the most common response, both of which were above the results for enterprises that collected income only, or income and rent.

As seen in figure 3.14, the second survey revealed that Roman Catholic churches were the leading denomination for church-based economic enterprises, which is likely due to the Roman Catholic church's history of providing private education in the United States. Roman Catholic churches were followed by nondenominational churches.

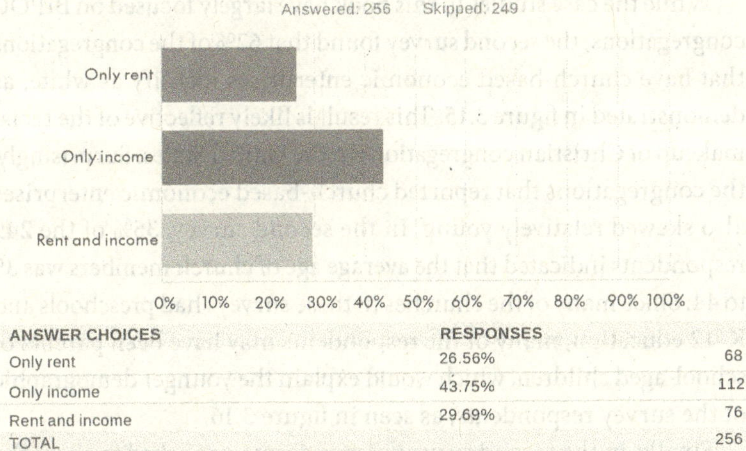

ANSWER CHOICES	RESPONSES	
Only rent	26.56%	68
Only income	43.75%	112
Rent and income	29.69%	76
TOTAL		256

Figure 3.13. Survey #2, Question 9: Rent or Income.
Source: Church-Based Economic Enterprises Survey, August 31, 2024, n=505.

Q11 How would you describe your congregation?

Answered: 249 Skipped: 256

Roman Catholic
Lutheran
Episcopal
Southern Baptist
Baptist
UCC
Nondenominational

0% 10% 20% 30% 40% 50% 60% 70% 80% 90% 100%

ANSWER CHOICES	RESPONSES	
Roman Catholic	34.94%	87
Lutheran	14.06%	35
Episcopal	5.62%	14
Southern Baptist	10.84%	27
Baptist	14.06%	35
UCC	0.80%	2
Nondenominational	19.68%	49
TOTAL		249

Figure 3.14. Survey #2, Question 11: Denominational Affiliations.
Source: Church-Based Economic Enterprises Survey, August 31, 2024, n=505.

While the case studies in this book have largely focused on BIPOC congregations, the second survey found that 62% of the congregations that have church-based economic enterprises identify as white, as demonstrated in figure 3.15. This result is likely reflective of the racial makeup of Christian congregations in the United States. Surprisingly, the congregations that reported church-based economic enterprises also skewed relatively young. In the second survey, 35% of the 249 respondents indicated that the average age of church members was 35 to 44. Since many of the churches in these surveys had preschools and K–12 education, many of the respondents may have been parents of school-aged children, which would explain the younger demographic of the survey respondents, as seen in figure 3.16.

Finally, in the second survey, respondents were asked to share the name and location of their church. Only 42 of the 159 respondents felt comfortable sharing this information, even though the survey assured confidentiality of the information. Of those 42 respondents,

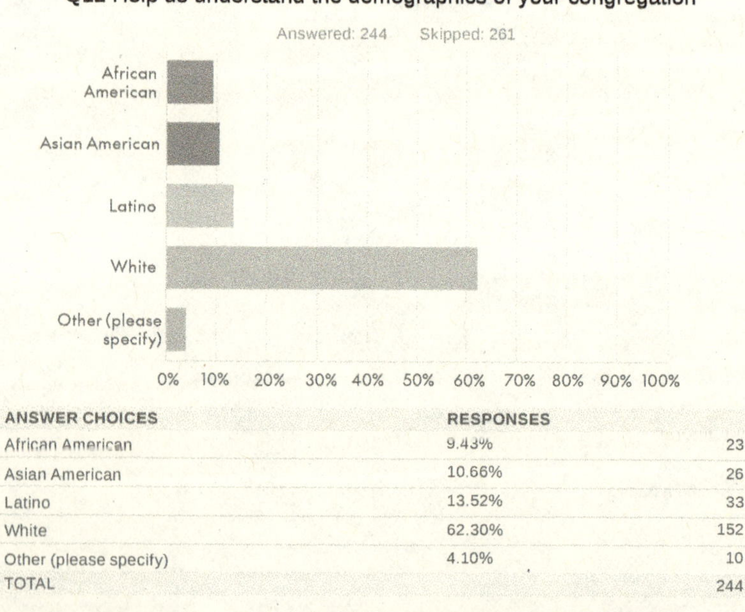

ANSWER CHOICES	RESPONSES	
African American	9.43%	23
Asian American	10.66%	26
Latino	13.52%	33
White	62.30%	152
Other (please specify)	4.10%	10
TOTAL		244

Figure 3.15. Survey #2, Question 12: Congregational Ethnicity.
Source: Church-Based Economic Enterprises Survey, August 31, 2024, n=505.

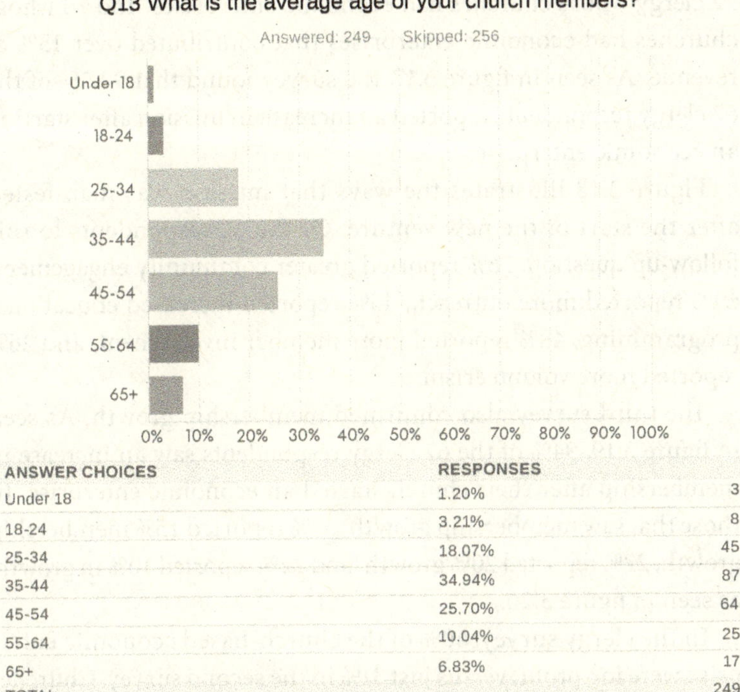

ANSWER CHOICES	RESPONSES	
Under 18	1.20%	3
18-24	3.21%	8
25-34	18.07%	45
35-44	34.94%	87
45-54	25.70%	64
55-64	10.04%	25
65+	6.83%	17
TOTAL		249

Figure 3.16. Survey #2, Question 13: Age of Congregation.
Source: Church-Based Economic Enterprises Survey, August 31, 2024, n=505.

all of them had nonprofit economic enterprises, and 86% (36 respondents) reported missional and membership growth after starting the economic enterprise, which is higher than the overall results in the second survey. In investigating those 42 churches, I could confirm the economic enterprises reported by 25 of the respondents in the survey. Surprisingly, many of the churches had more than one economic enterprise. The question had only provided for one answer, but in the follow-up research, it was clear that many congregations have multiple church-based economic ventures. For example, most of the Roman Catholic churches that had a K–8 school also had a preschool. Many of the large nondenominational churches that had a coffee shop also had a store that sold church-related merchandise, like hats and T-shirts.

The third survey was conducted on September 6, 2024, through SurveyMonkey. The survey started with 122 respondents to find

72 clergy whose churches had economic enterprises, and 70 whose churches had economic enterprises that contributed over 15% of revenue. As seen in figure 3.17, the survey found that 92.5% of the 67 clergy respondents reported an increase in mission after starting an economic enterprise.

Figure 3.18 illustrates the ways that mission was manifested after the start of the new venture. Of the 62 respondents to this follow-up question, 76% reported greater community engagement, 69% reported more outreach, 45% reported increased educational programming, 48% reported more member involvement, and 26% reported more volunteerism.

The third survey also confirmed membership growth. As seen in figure 3.19, 94% of the 67 clergy respondents saw an increase in membership after their church started an economic enterprise. In those that saw membership growth, 38% reported 15% membership growth, 22% reported 20% growth, and 22% reported 10% in growth, as seen in figure 3.20.

In the clergy survey, 60% of the church-based economic enterprise were for-profit, versus just 31% in the second survey. Churches with for-profit economic enterprises experienced more missional

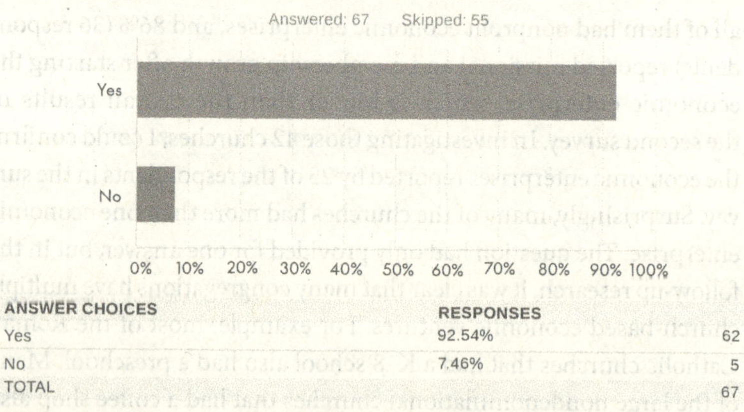

ANSWER CHOICES	RESPONSES	
Yes	92.54%	62
No	7.46%	5
TOTAL		67

Figure 3.17. Survey #3, Question 6: Missional Increase.
Source: Church-Based Economic Enterprises Survey, September 6, 2024, n=122.

Q7 How has the missional renewal manifested at your church?

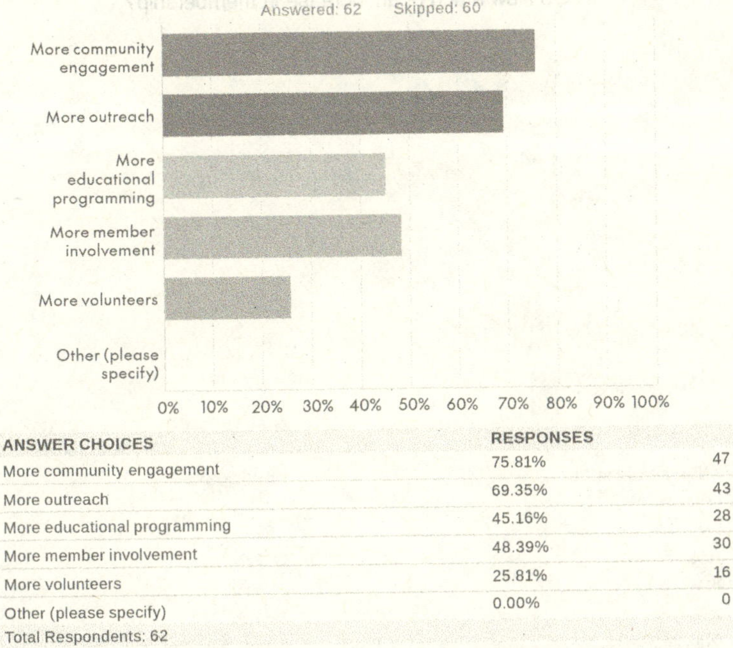

ANSWER CHOICES	RESPONSES	
More community engagement	75.81%	47
More outreach	69.35%	43
More educational programming	45.16%	28
More member involvement	48.39%	30
More volunteers	25.81%	16
Other (please specify)	0.00%	0
Total Respondents: 62		

Figure 3.18. Survey #3, Question 7: Types of Missional Increase.
Source: Church-Based Economic Enterprises Survey, September 6, 2024, n=122.

Q4 Have you experienced an increase in membership since opening the economic enterprise?

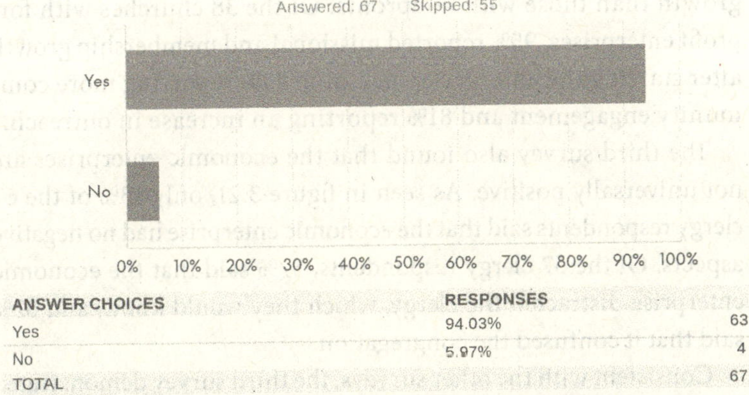

ANSWER CHOICES	RESPONSES	
Yes	94.03%	63
No	5.97%	4
TOTAL		67

Figure 3.19. Survey #3, Question 4: Membership Increase.
Source: Church-Based Economic Enterprises Survey, September 6, 2024, n=122.

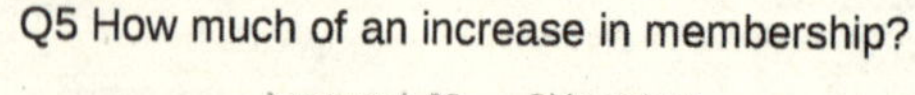

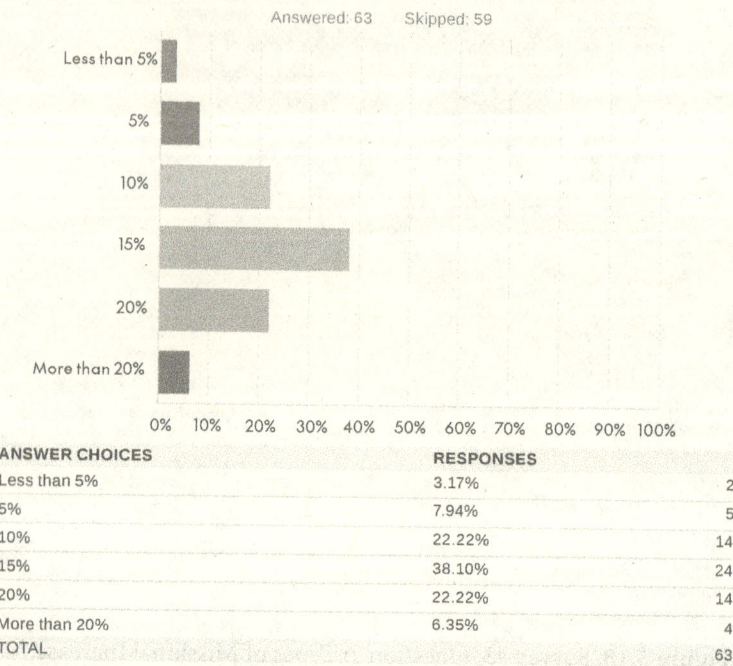

ANSWER CHOICES	RESPONSES	
Less than 5%	3.17%	2
5%	7.94%	5
10%	22.22%	14
15%	38.10%	24
20%	22.22%	14
More than 20%	6.35%	4
TOTAL		63

Figure 3.20. Survey #3, Question 5: Amount of Membership Increase. **Source:** Church-Based Economic Enterprises Survey, September 6, 2024, n=122.

growth than those with nonprofits. Of the 38 churches with for-profit enterprises, 95% reported missional and membership growth after starting the enterprise, including 83% reporting more community engagement and 81% reporting an increase in outreach.

The third survey also found that the economic enterprises are not universally positive. As seen in figure 3.21, only 13% of the 67 clergy respondents said that the economic enterprise had no negative aspects. Of the 67 clergy respondents, 57% said that the economic enterprise distracted the clergy, which they would know, and 52% said that it confused the congregation.

Consistent with the other surveys, the third survey demonstrated the overwhelmingly positive impact of church-based economic enterprises on missional renewal and congregational growth. In addition,

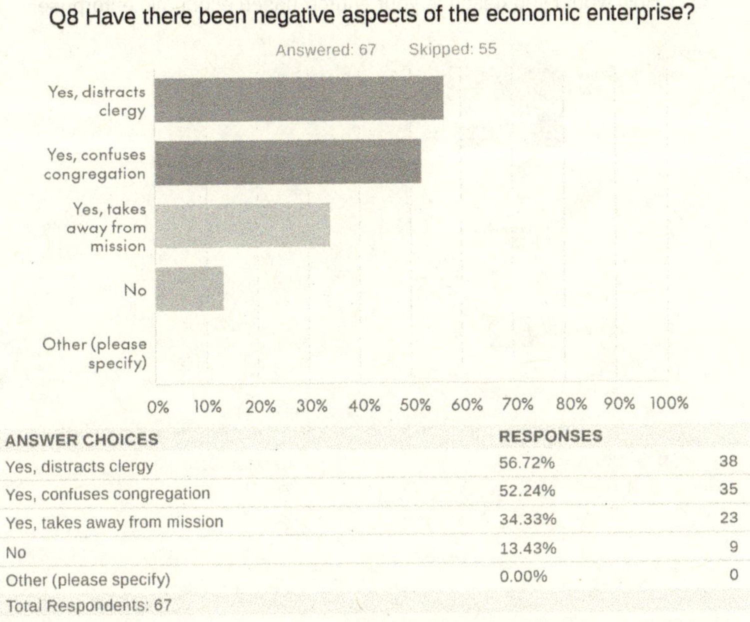

ANSWER CHOICES	RESPONSES	
Yes, distracts clergy	56.72%	38
Yes, confuses congregation	52.24%	35
Yes, takes away from mission	34.33%	23
No	13.43%	9
Other (please specify)	0.00%	0
Total Respondents: 67		

Figure 3.21. Survey #3, Question 8: Negative Aspects of Economic Enterprises.
Source: Church-Based Economic Enterprises Survey, September 6, 2024, n=122.

the third survey asked about the details of the economic enterprise and the demographics of the congregation. As seen in figure 3.22, the survey revealed that preschools and day care were the most common business, followed by thrift shops and then coffee shops, which was consistent with the results from the second survey.

In analyzing the data about the different types of economic enterprises, figure 3.23 describes the missional and congregational growth experienced from the impact of those different enterprises. In figure 3.23, the second column reports the percentage of congregations that reported missional growth. The third column reports the percentage of congregations that reported growth in membership after starting that type of economic enterprise. The fourth column is the most frequent membership growth reported associated with that type of economic enterprise. Based on these findings, preschools and day

Q11 How would you describe your church-based economic enterprise?

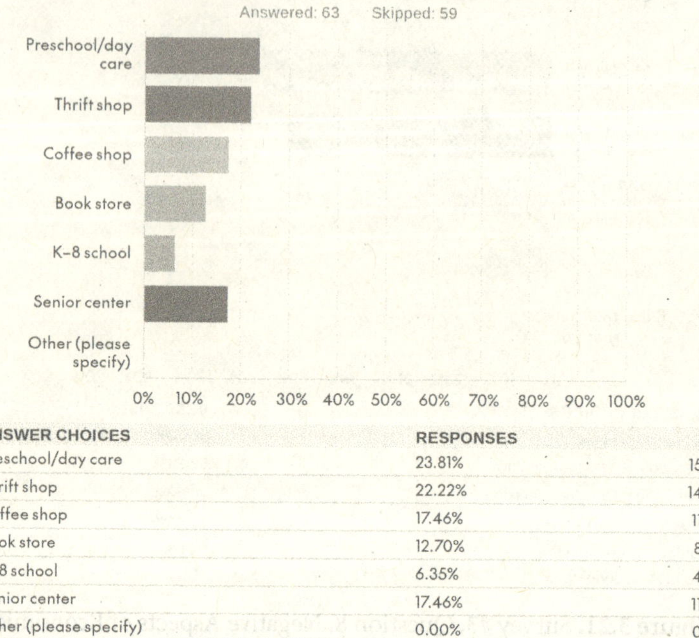

ANSWER CHOICES	RESPONSES	
Preschool/day care	23.81%	15
Thrift shop	22.22%	14
Coffee shop	17.46%	11
Book store	12.70%	8
K–8 school	6.35%	4
Senior center	17.46%	11
Other (please specify)	0.00%	0
TOTAL		63

Figure 3.22. Survey #3, Question 11: Describe Your Church-Based Economic Enterprise.

Source: Church-Based Economic Enterprises Survey, September 6, 2024, n=122.

Economic Enterprise	Missional Growth (%)	Membership Growth (%)	Growth Rate (%)
Preschool/Day care	100	100	15
Thrift shop	86	93	15
Coffee shop	91	91	15–20
Book store	100	100	15
K–8 school	75	75	20+
Senior center	91	91	5

Figure 3.23. Survey #3, Chart 1: Types of Economic Enterprises and Growth Rates.

Source: Church-Based Economic Enterprises Survey, September 6, 2024, n=122.

care are the most likely enterprises to drive missional and membership growth. For the best overall membership growth, churches with K–8 schools saw the strongest growth in membership, reporting 20% growth. However, only 75% of churches with K–8 schools reported any growth in membership at all, which is the smallest among the economic enterprises included in the survey. The second survey also revealed this same trend in K–8 schools. It was surprising how many churches had started one of the six economic enterprises listed in Figure 3.23. These are fairly traditional enterprises for churches, and as the survey shows, they yield great benefits in member and missional growth.

In addition, as seen in figure 3.24, the survey found that churches that just collect rent also see strong growth from the economic enterprises that are started on their campuses. Of the 17 respondents that only collected rent, and not additional income, 88% saw missional growth and 88% saw membership growth, with 15% growth as the most common response, both of which were lower than the overall results for the third survey.

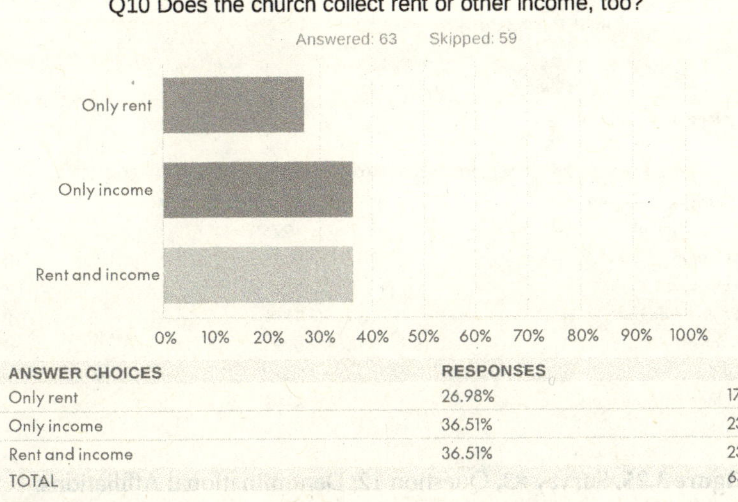

ANSWER CHOICES	RESPONSES	
Only rent	26.98%	17
Only income	36.51%	23
Rent and income	36.51%	23
TOTAL		63

Figure 3.24. Survey #3, Question 10: Rent or Income.
Source: Church-Based Economic Enterprises Survey, September 6, 2024, n=122.

Consistent with the second survey, figure 3.25 illustrates that the clergy survey revealed that Roman Catholic churches were the leading denomination for church-based economic enterprises, which is likely due to the Roman Catholic church's history of providing private education in the United States.

This survey found that 78% of the congregations that have church-based economic enterprises identify as white, as seen in figure 3.26. Surprisingly, the congregations that reported church-based economic enterprises also skewed relatively young, as seen in figure 3.27. In the third survey, 36% of the 64 respondents indicated that the average age of church members was 35 to 44.

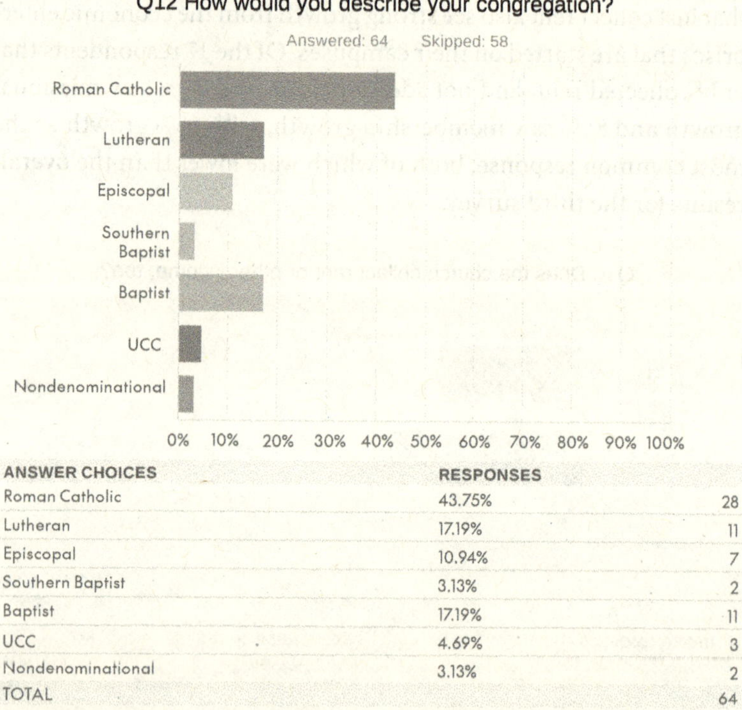

ANSWER CHOICES	RESPONSES	
Roman Catholic	43.75%	28
Lutheran	17.19%	11
Episcopal	10.94%	7
Southern Baptist	3.13%	2
Baptist	17.19%	11
UCC	4.69%	3
Nondenominational	3.13%	2
TOTAL		64

Figure 3.25. Survey #3, Question 12: Denominational Affiliations. **Source:** Church-Based Economic Enterprises Survey, September 6, 2024, n=122.

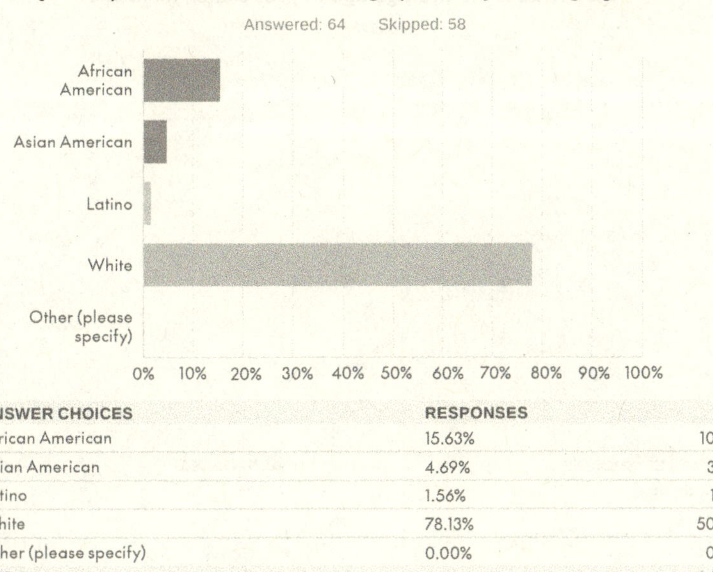

ANSWER CHOICES	RESPONSES	
African American	15.63%	10
Asian American	4.69%	3
Latino	1.56%	1
White	78.13%	50
Other (please specify)	0.00%	0
TOTAL		64

Figure 3.26. Survey #3, Question 13: Congregational Ethnicity.
Source: Church-Based Economic Enterprises Survey, September 6, 2024, n=122.

Finally, in the clergy survey, respondents were asked to share the name and location of their church. In the survey, only five respondents provided this information. In investigating those five churches, I could confirm the economic enterprises reported by the respondents in the survey. Of those five respondents, all of them had nonprofit economic enterprises, and 80% (four respondents) reported missional and membership growth after starting the economic enterprise, which is lower than the overall results in the third survey. Also, as in the second survey, many of the churches that provided their name and location had multiple enterprises. Perhaps as churches become more comfortable starting and operating an economic enterprise, they become more comfortable at introducing additional ones.

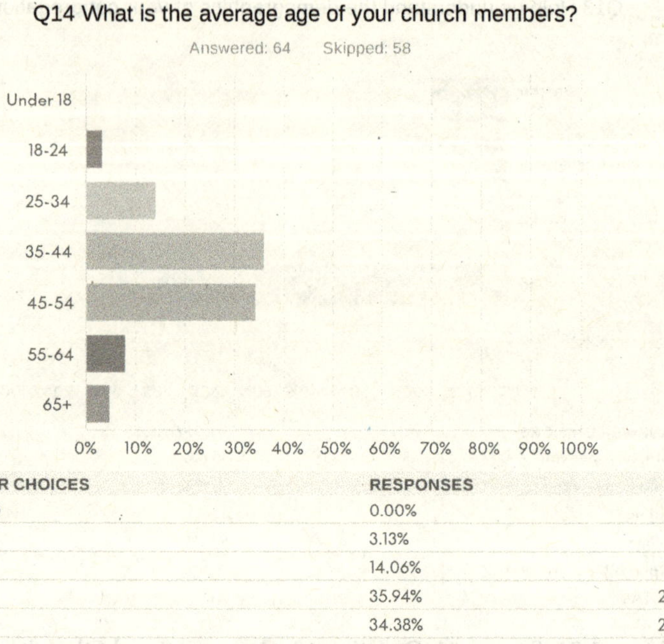

ANSWER CHOICES	RESPONSES	
Under 18	0.00%	0
18-24	3.13%	2
25-34	14.06%	9
35-44	35.94%	23
45-54	34.38%	22
55-64	7.81%	5
65+	4.69%	3
TOTAL		64

Figure 3.27. Survey #3, Question 14: Age of Congregation.
Source: Church-Based Economic Enterprises Survey, September 6, 2024, n=122.

CHAPTER 4

Best Practices and Practical Theology

As described in the introduction, this book has set out to answer four questions:

1. What do church-based economic enterprises have to do with discipleship and missiology?
2. How can churches change their missional and financial models?
3. Can church-based economic enterprises have any impact on missional vitality or congregational growth?
4. What is the role for practical theology in fostering church-based economic enterprises?

As the case studies in this book demonstrate, church-based economic enterprises can lead to missional renewal, congregational growth, advancements in social justice, and an alternative to the current economic system. The case studies also illustrate how church-based economic enterprises can provide opportunities for people who have been kept from owning or operating enterprises. These businesses can be decolonial because they include people on the economic and social margin, and they support economic ventures that are delinked from historical economic powers. Economic globalism will characterize these local businesses as ineffective and noncompetitive, but they are demonstrating otherwise. Moreover, they are proving that economic activity does not always need to be conducted in-line with the current economic status quo. By providing these economic alternatives, these congregations are also renewing a sense of individual and communal agency. As a result, the benefits for these economic enterprises extend beyond the church and the entrepreneurs to the entire community. These communities are seeing multiple forms of renewal. They are developing new parks, new community centers, and new political power.

The case studies also illustrate that it is possible to change missional and financial models. In fact, the challenge to current church financial models provides an opportunity for churches to review and renew their mission. The financial crisis can catalyze a transition from an ecclesiological focus to a missional focus. Moreover, the three surveys included above demonstrate that church-based economic enterprises can clearly lead to missional renewal and membership growth. While it is difficult to measure missional renewal, survey respondents reported increases in community engagement, outreach, educational programming, member involvement, and volunteerism, all of which are good indicators of the *missio Dei*. Moreover, when visiting the congregations in the case studies, they had a clear sense of renewed energy and agency, which was not limited to the church but extended to the entire neighborhood.

The case studies also highlight eight best practices that mark successful changes in missional and financial models:

1. **The primary focus must be missional, not financial.** In all four case studies, the churches began by examining the needs in their community. They focused on mission, which subsequently led to helping develop economic enterprises that truly served their communities and their mission. Their work with economic enterprises ultimately had modest financial benefits. However, the financial benefits were largely tertiary. The primary and secondary benefits were missional renewal and congregation growth. These

enterprises also enhanced their missions by advancing social justice and offering economic alternatives to conventional capitalism. In addition, once they started one venture, it was easy to start another one. In following up with the congregations that responded to the surveys, it was surprising how many congregations operated multiple economic ventures, both for-profit and nonprofit.

2. **A clergy person does not need a business background or entrepreneurial experience to start new businesses.** None of the leaders in the case studies knew anything about the businesses that developed in their congregations. Through asset assessment and community listening, they found their mission, and their mission took them outside of the church. Like any good entrepreneur, these leaders needed the courage to try something new and to move out of their comfort zone.
3. **Leaders need to be committed for the long term.** At the time of this writing in 2025, Pastor Randolph has twenty years at his congregation. Pastor Ferguson has sixteen years at her congregation. Pastor John Cummins has ten years at GIA and Meghan Sobocienski has ten years at GIAC. The Rev. Ciosek has eleven years at his parish. In addition, these congregations have several long-term lay leaders. Pastor Randolph's Senior Warden Tamika Hamilton has been active at the Church of the Messiah for decades. I have only served my own parish for six years, but we have launched an economic enterprise because of the strong foundation that was laid by lay and clerical leaders before me.
4. **All leaders must be willing to experiment with new models of mission, including new financial models.** Even if the first economic venture is unsuccessful, the lessons learned will serve the congregation in the future if it tries other enterprises. More important, the church can demonstrate the importance of experimentation to all its congregants, which might make them more willing to do it. Colonial

thinking seeks to limit the imagination of those under its subjugation. Therefore, experimentation and imagination are deeply decolonial and also essential to the *missio Dei.*

5. **Active lay leadership is essential.** All four of the case studies relied upon and continue to rely upon lay leaders. Clergy cannot make these transitions on their own. Moreover, clergy should see this work as an opportunity to encourage individual and communal agency. In the case studies, the clergy were not running these businesses, but helping people to start them, and then they were stepping away.
6. **Mission emerges from supporting people on the margins.** In these case studies, the churches provide support for people who are or have historically been exploited by the current economic systems. As an act of faith and mission, these congregations resist the current economic systems of oppression by creating economic opportunities for historically marginalized people. In the surveys completed for this book, church-based economic enterprises were not primarily led by, and did not primarily benefit, the BIPOC community. In the surveys, the overwhelming majority of the congregations leading church-based economic enterprises are white. Yet, even in white congregations, like St. Peter's Episcopal Church in Dartmouth, Massachusetts, the congregations serve people who have largely been overlooked or ignored.
7. **These congregations know their local ecosystem.** In fact, in the surveys, enhanced community engagement was one of the primary benefits of church-based economic ventures. It is unlikely that a venture will succeed unless someone fully understands the local ecosystem. For that, the congregation needs to be engaged with the community outside of the church. Therefore, understanding the local ecosystem is another way of assuring that the church is moving outside of its building and fully engaging in the

community. It aids the transition from an ecclesiological focus to a missiological one.

8. **Faith and mission must be at the center.** In all four case studies, there is a consistent link to faith and mission. People attend Sunday services because of the missional work that these churches are doing the rest of the week. By leading with missional work, these churches have developed healthy congregational and solid financial models. They demonstrate that economic enterprises need not be a distraction from faith, but rather a way of reinforcing faith and a basis for faith formation throughout a congregation and a community.

In these four case studies and in three surveys, the churches are reaching out in mission. They are trying to understand how they are called to bring the gospel into the world. They focus on community formation, and the interpretation of Scripture and actions, which results in the call for new business formation. They demonstrate that church-based economic enterprises are a bold expression of the *missio Dei*. These new enterprises reflect theological and missional concepts in their specific social context. The churches recognize that they are empowering all God's children by helping people to develop their own ventures and to achieve economic independence. In fact, there is also evidence that they are empowering people beyond the church. These communities have seen revitalization because of the churches' work on economic development. At the same time, these churches are underscoring that all God's people are part of the body of Christ and the *missio Dei*. While the churches may not ultimately control these economic enterprises, they can offer active formation and moral guidance. The case studies in this book prove that an economic enterprise can focus on employee benefits and environmental impact, rather than executive compensation, profit maximization, and capital accumulation. They embody what an economic enterprise looks like when it takes the gospel and mission seriously. Going forward, there is an opportunity for churches to develop more specific ethical guidelines for the businesses that they operate or those that they incubate in their facilities. Finally, through formation and support, these churches are reminding both Christians and non-Christians that the "Christian life" exists outside the walls of the church. They are showing people what it means to be active Christian disciples and to live into Christian mission. They are also helping all churches see that their futures are missional, rather than ecclesiological. They demonstrate that church-based economic enterprises can help churches to do well by doing good. They are part of the *missio Dei.*

Chapter 1 referenced Audre Lorde's observation that "the master's tools will never dismantle the master's house."[1] These economic enterprises may look at lot like the master's tools. However, in these case studies, the tools are not necessarily dismantling the master's house but enabling people to build something new. Eventually, the master will start to feel threatened, but currently, the economic enterprises described in this book are too small to capture attention. Over time, church-based economic enterprises will start to impact competitive market dynamics, and then they will receive much more attention. Therefore, new church-based enterprises will need to prepare to resist the master's retaliation, which will be critical to advancing the *missio Dei* in the midst of these challenges. Practical theologians James Poling and Donald Miller argue that practical theology is evidenced in communities of faith reaching out in mission. For them, ministry should be primarily focused on community formation and interpretation of community faith traditions for the congregation.[2] So, there will be more work to do, more economic challenges to consider, and more ethical questions to evaluate. But, with the creative power of the Holy Spirit and the congregational energy of these new ventures, we will be able to face those challenges and boldly continue the work of the *missio Dei.*

Postlude

Putting It All Together—St. Francis of Assisi Episcopal Church

Based on the research for this book, my own parish, St. Francis of Assisi Episcopal Church (SF), began discerning upon starting an economic enterprise. In early 2025, SF partnered with an adult respite care provider to launch a nonprofit respite care business. It has been very hard work. However, even though the enterprise had just launched at the time of this writing, the discernment process alone has been incredibly helpful. I would wholeheartedly recommend it. At SF, the discernment involved three stages: congregational review, discernment on economic enterprises generally, and discernment on the types of economic enterprises that our congregation could pursue.

For our congregational review, I returned to some congregation exercises that we had completed previously. These exercises asked people to mark on a chart where they think the church is in its congregational life cycle. People were asked to identify their two most important forms of Anglican spirituality and Anglican temperament. The exercises reinforced the congregation's understanding of itself and confirmed its stability. As a result, we were able to discern that it was an appropriate time to start a conversation about an enterprise.

At our annual meeting in January 2023, I described my thoughts about creating an economic enterprise at SF. At the meeting, there was an enthusiastic response. I developed an ad hoc discernment committee. I had hoped to have some naysayers on the committee who did not think starting an economic enterprise would be a good idea. I wanted to hear a diversity of voices from this congregation. Over two years later, I still have not heard any objections to an economic enterprise.

The committee had its first meeting on February 18, 2023. We had nine people attend, and they represented a diverse set of backgrounds of our congregation. I started the meeting with some quiet and with a song by Audrey Assad, *I Shall Not Want*. Both Parker Palmer and Elizabeth Liebert have stressed the importance of silence and faith-sharing in initiating any discernment process.[1] After playing the song, I asked people why I would have chosen it. They understood that we were approaching this economic enterprise not from a position of want or dire need, but as an expression of our faith and mission. We agreed that this economic initiative must be an expression of the *missio Dei*. Our initial meeting created a lot of enthusiasm. Several people who attended the meeting emailed me afterward to express their excitement about this project.

We continued to meet monthly until we reached a consensus on our direction. The initial meetings were so productive because everyone participated in them. They all felt free to share their views, and the conversation kept growing. More important, two people took on two follow-up activities in preparation for our subsequent meetings. One person investigated the Trappist monks' tradition of operating economic enterprises in their communities, and another explored adult and child day care facilities in our area. It was encouraging to see people taking ownership for this project so quickly.[2]

In this discernment work, we focused on widening the purpose and mission of an economic venture, and we looked to demonstrate the ways in which an economic enterprise would reinforce the mission of SF.[3] Currently, the church's stated mission is "to know Christ, to worship Christ, to serve Christ." If a new economic initiative did not advance our mission, then it was unlikely to be sustainable. Therefore, we continued to ask theologically reflective questions as we engaged in this discernment process.[4] For example, during one of our initial meetings, we discussed what it meant to be a Christian business. We developed a list of actions we, as leaders of a gospel-based economic enterprise, should take:

1. Do not proselytize, sermonize, or ask for a quid pro quo.
2. Practice integrity: offer fair wages and fair prices, and practice creation care.
3. Follow the Golden Rule: Do as to others as you would like done to you.
4. Ask, What would St. Francis do? (WWFD).
5. Commit to quality and aesthetics.
6. Make cash-flow positive over time.
7. Maintain an ethic of sufficiency and be watchful about indulgent spending.
8. Provide an example for others of what a "Christian business" or "gospel-based business" looks like.
9. Reinforce the St. Francis brand.
10. Increase our presence in and commitment to the wider community.
11. Be an example of Christian discipleship.
12. Do not be pompous twits.

Early on, we also recognized that we needed a communication plan. Communication shows respect and inclusion. It also demonstrates listening by the leaders. Communications in church frequently requires overcommunicating because people generally do not pay close attention to them. There need to be multiple venues for sharing information. Therefore, I posted our meeting minutes, updated our vestry monthly, provided updates by email and in our newsletter, and shared information about our economic enterprise with the congregation at Sunday services.

After our opening process, we had two presentations about potential businesses. The first presentation was about adult day care facilities. The second presentation described a faith-based retail boutique.

Both ideas generated strong interest. In our discussion of the adult day care, we thought about creating intergenerational opportunities by locating an adult day care close to a children's day care. Following the meeting, another committee member and I started investigating where there might be retail space available for both these ideas and what the pricing might be for them. While it was just the very initial stages, we started to do a little practical research.

In one of our early meetings, we started the meeting by considering SF's core values: faithfulness, respect, care, integrity, and collaboration. We started to consider our business opportunities in-line with those values. The exercise provided a way for theological reflection as we continued our discernment. We also began to investigate the regulatory, funding, and staffing requirements for an adult day care. Coming out of the meeting, several committee members agreed to investigate additional aspects of an adult day care. In addition, as we began our investigation, we prioritized maintaining a degree of spiritual detachment, so that the Holy Spirit could guide our process rather than our own ideas and egos.

By fall 2023, we began envisioning a pilot project for an adult day care or respite care program, St. Francis Respite Care (SFRC). It would provide nonmedical support, including social activities and minor health monitoring to older adults. It would be operated three afternoons per week out of the parish hall. It would be staffed with limited medical personnel, and initially, it would not serve people suffering from Alzheimer's or significant cognitive impairment. Over time, SFRC might consider more complex patients with more demanding medical needs. It might also expand its hours of operation. The primary beneficiaries would be adults in need of short-term, nonmedical care outside of the home, and perhaps more important, their caregivers. Within the adult care industry, this limited, nonmedical care is commonly called "respite care," because it provides rest for both the individual in need of care and for their caregiver. According to a 2018 report from the Administration for Community Living, respite care provides relief to caregivers.[5] As a result, they can avoid burnout, and the person in need of care can avoid costly institutionalization.

Caregiving has also become more demanding as families have shrunk in size, leaving fewer family members to provide care. Nora Super, executive director of the Milken Institute Center for the Future of Aging, notes that in the past, the "traditional ratio of caregivers to older adults was seven-to-one," but with smaller families, that ratio is expected to shrink to four-to-one by 2030.[6] Super also notes that the BIPOC community is particularly impacted by the limited availability of respite care.[7] In 2000, the US Congress passed the National Family Caregiver Support Program, which provides "funding through grants to private and voluntary agencies that assist family caregivers with services, including respite."[8] The legislation recognizes the economic value of in-home care that is provided by a family member or loved one, rather than much more expensive institutional care. Based on the success of respite care, the US Congress provided additional funding and support in the RAISE Family Caregivers Act in January 2018.[9]

According to the US Centers for Disease Control and Prevention, there are 4,127 adult day services centers in the United States, and they serve 237,400 people on any given day.[10] Also, 45% of the adult day service centers are for-profit facilities.[11] SFRC is currently registered as a nonprofit. Nonmedical adult day services centers, like SFRC, serve an average of 34.2 people per day and run at 51.3% of their capacity.[12] Based on Oregon regulations, SFRC could serve up to 30 people in the St. Francis parish hall. According to the US National Center for Health Statistics, nonmedical adult day services are largely covered by Medicaid. Medicaid accounts for 47.2% of the costs, but individuals pay 16.9%. The remaining costs may be covered by other state, federal and local government programs, including the US Veterans Administration.[13]

The SFRC pilot project has enabled our community to test the business model and the demand for the service. Initially, we had developed a business plan. We had secured nonprofit status, and we were registered as a nonprofit corporation. We filed articles of incorporation and bylaws. We had also applied for grants to fund a director for the program. We envisioned that once we had one year's salary secured for the director, we would start to recruit one. In addition, before a formal launch, we knew that we would need to establish a bank account and means of paying for our services, like a credit card and Venmo. In Oregon, we are not required to be licensed as an adult care facility to offer our services. However, our goal was to be fully licensed. Once licensed, SFRC could accept Medicare and Medicaid for its services.

Suddenly, in December 2024, we had a call from a woman who was looking to start an adult respite care program in Wilsonville. She reached out to us because she had contacted the local senior center, which knew of our plans. The woman who contacted us is a nurse with expertise in geriatric psychology and over ten years of experience providing respite care. We would not have found a better partner. So, in early 2025 SF leased two thousand square feet of its parish hall to this woman and her business to operate a nonprofit respite care program. Initially, the lease was for just one year, so that our congregation could see what it meant to really share our space with another. There is some uneasiness about these changes, but there is also excitement. We have held two congregational meetings to meet our new partner and to field questions and comments about the program.

Over two years ago, SF began a discernment process considering whether we could start an economic enterprise, and now we have found a partner and we have launched one. In our past meetings and moving forward, we have relied heavily upon Elizabeth Liebert's discernment guidelines. Looking ahead, I am expecting that we may need to wait for our answers. Our practice with compassion-based strategic discernment in this case will help us in all our future discernment needs. Ultimately, regardless of the outcome of this new venture, SF is called to grow in its ability to discern together and individually to advance the *mission Dei*. This work helps us to ultimately "live discerningly until we develop habitually listening hearts and lives responsive to God's call to us as individuals and communities."[14] Discernment helps us all to better understand our agency in relation to God and the ways in which God's call us all to flourishing and thriving, which seems to be the core mission of all our work as Jesus's disciples, whether we are starting economic enterprises, leading worship services or quietly contemplating the blessings of this life.[15] They embrace the *missio Dei*.

Our work at SF has hardly even started, and it has taken us over two years just to get to this point. There have been distractions and obstacles along the way. We remain inspired by the case studies in this book. They, too, faced uncertainty and distraction, but they stuck to their work, and they have done amazing things in their communities and congregations. They have lived into the *missio Dei* and moved their communities closer to being God's Beloved Community. At SF, we are merely trying to do the same.

Notes

INTRODUCTION

1 Gerald W. Keucher, *Remember the Future: Financial Leadership and Asset Management for Congregations* (Church Publishing, 2006), 134.
2 Drew Lindsay, "'Pretty Scary': 7 Things to Know About Religion's Decline and Charitable Giving," *The Chronicle of Philanthropy*, December 12, 2023.
3 James N. Poling and Donald E. Miller, *Foundations for a Practical Theology of Ministry* (Abington, 1985), 61.
4 Poling and Miller, *Foundations*, 62.
5 Walter Brueggemann, *Money and Possessions* (Westminster John Knox Press, 2016), xix.
6 Michael Schut, ed., *Money & Faith: The Search for Enough* (Morehouse Publishing, 2008), 39.
7 Schut, *Money & Faith*, 39.
8 Brueggemann, *Money and Possessions*, 5.
9 Brueggemann, *Money and Possessions*, 53.
10 Brueggemann, *Money and Possessions*, 36.
11 Brueggemann, *Money and Possessions*, 49.
12 Brueggemann, *Money and Possessions*, 49.
13 Brueggemann, *Money and Possessions*, 99.
14 Brueggemann, *Money and Possessions*, 114.
15 Brueggemann, *Money and Possessions*, 187.
16 Justo L. González, *Faith and Wealth: A History of Early Christian Ideas on the Origin, Significance and Use of Money* (Wipf & Stock, 1990), 78.
17 Luke Timothy Johnson, *Sharing Possessions: What Faith Demands*, 2nd ed. (Eerdmans, 2011), 19.
18 Sondra Ely Wheeler, *Wealth as Peril and Obligation* (Eerdmans, 1995), 46.
19 González, *Faith and Wealth*, 76.
20 González, *Faith and Wealth*, 93.
21 González, *Faith and Wealth*, 95.
22 González, *Faith and Wealth*, 113.
23 González, *Faith and Wealth*, 101.

24 Brian J. Matz, "The Principle of Detachment from Private Propery in Basil of Caesarea's Homily 6 and Its Context," in *Reading Patristic Texts on Social Ethics*, ed. Johan Leemans, Brian J. Matz and Johan Verstraeten (Catholic University of America Press, 2011), 183.
25 Peter Brown, *Through the Eye of a Needle: Wealth, the Fall of Rome and the Making of Christianity in the West, 350–550 AD* (Princeton University Press, 2012), 8.
26 González, *Faith and Wealth*, 231.
27 González, *Faith and Wealth*, 111.
28 Matz, "Principle of Detachment," 183.
29 Harvey Cox, *The Market as God* (Harvard University Press, 2016), 139.
30 Brown, *Through the Eye of a Needle*, 530.
31 Benedict, *The Holy Rule of St. Benedict*, 1949 ed., trans. Boniface Verheyen, accessed September 26, 2024, https://www.catholicspiritualdirection.org/rulebenedict.pdf.
32 Thomas Aquinas. *Summa Theologica*, 2–2.77.1, https://www.ccel.org/a/aquinas/summa/SS/SS077.html#SSQ77OUTP1.
33 Esther Chung-Kim and Todd R. Hains, *Reformation Commentary on Scripture: Acts* (IVP Academic, 2014), 158.
34 Paul Wesley Chilcote, ed., *John & Charles Wesley: Selections from Their Writings and Hymns—Annotated & Explained* (Skylight Paths Publishing, 2011), 238–39.
35 Benjamin M. Friedman, *Religion and the Rise of Capitalism* (Vintage Books, 2022), 307.
36 Eugene McCarraher, *The Enchantments of Mammon: How Capitalism Became the Religion of Modernity* (Belknap Press of Harvard University Press, 2019), 351, 353.
37 Christine Firer Hinze, "What is Enough?" in *Having: Property and Possession in Religious and Social Life*, eds. William Schweiker and Charles Mathewes (Eerdmans, 2004), 169.
38 Ignacio Ellacuría, *Ignacio Ellacuría: Essays on History, Liberation and Salvation*, ed. and trans. Michael E. Lee (Orbis, 2013), 110.
39 Ellacuría, *Ignacio Ellacuría*, 52.
40 Ellacuría, *Ignacio Ellacuría*, 129.
41 Ellacuría, *Ignacio Ellacuría*, 134.
42 Ellacuría, *Ignacio Ellacuría* 130.

CHAPTER 1: PRACTICAL THEOLOGY OF ECONOMICS

1 Poling and Miller, *Foundations*, 63.
2 Poling and Miller, *Foundations*, 11.
3 Poling and Miller, *Foundations*, 13.
4 Richard Osmer, *Practical Theology: An Introduction* (Eerdmans, 2008), 8.

5 Mark Elsdon, *We Aren't Broke: Uncovering Hidden Resources for Mission and Ministry* (Eerdmans, 2021), 8.
6 John P. Kretzmann and John L. McKnight, *Building Communities from the Inside Out: A Path Toward Finding and Mobilizing a Community's Assets* (Acta, 1993), 1, 5.
7 Lisa Lowe, *The Intimacies of Four Continents* (Duke University Press, 2015), 63–64; Walter D. Mignolo, "Delinking: The Rhetoric of Modernity, The Logic of Coloniality and The Grammar of De-Coloniality," in *Globalization and the Decolonial Option*, ed. Walter D. Mignolo and Arturo Escobar (Routledge, 2013) 327, 333.
8 David Harvey, *The Limits to Capital* (Verso, 218), 415.
9 Kate Bowler, *Blessed: A History of the American Prosperity Gospel* (Oxford University Press, 2018), 12.
10 Bowler, *Blessed*, 14.
11 Bowler, *Blessed*, 14.
12 Bowler, *Blessed*, 14.
13 Bowler, *Blessed*, 15.
14 Bowler, *Blessed*, 20.
15 Bowler, *Blessed*, 21, 26.
16 Janine Giordano Drake, *The Gospel of Church: How Mainline Protestants Vilified Christian Socialism and Fractured the Labor Movement* (Oxford University Press, 2024), 5.
17 Drake, *The Gospel of Church*, 15.
18 Carter Heyward, *The Seven Deadly Sins of White Christian Nationalism: A Call to Action* (Rowman & Littlefield, 2022), 106.
19 Bowler, *Blessed*, 60.
20 Bowler, *Blessed*, 77.
21 Bowler, *Blessed*, 77.
22 Bowler, *Blessed*, 96.
23 Bowler, *Blessed*, 99.
24 Bowler, *Blessed*, 126.
25 Bowler, *Blessed*, 126.
26 Bowler, *Blessed*, 136.
27 Bowler, *Blessed*, 181.
28 Bowler, *Blessed*, 193.
29 Bowler, *Blessed*, 193.
30 Bowler, *Blessed*, 201.
31 Bowler, *Blessed*, 201.
32 Joerg Rieger, *Theology in the Capitalocene: Ecology, Identity, Class and Solidarity* (Fortress, 2009), 60.
33 Heyward, *Seven Deadly Sins of White Christian Nationalism*, 108.
34 Heyward, *Seven Deadly Sins of White Christian Nationalism*, 115.
35 C. Neal Johnson, *Business as Mission: A Comprehensive Guide to Theory and Practice* (IVP Academic, 2011), 19.

36 Johnson, *Business as Mission*, 22.
37 Johnson, *Business as Mission*, 20.
38 Johnson, *Business as Mission*, 23.
39 David A. Bosch, "The Gap Between Best Practices and Actual Practices: A BAM Field Study," *Christian Business Academy Review* 12, no. 1, (Spring 2017): 33, https://doi.org/10.69492/cbar.v12i0.446.
40 Johnson, *Business as Mission*, 21.
41 Sello Moloi, "South African Telco Signs Deal with Local Church to Sell Phones to Its 7 Million Members," TNW, April 24, 2017, https://thenextweb.com/news/south-african-telco-partners-shembe-church-sell-phones-7m-members.
42 Emmanuel Y. Lartey, *Postcolonializing God: An African Practical Theology* (SCM Press, 2013), 5.
43 Frances M. Young and David F. Ford, *Meaning and Truth in Second Corinthians* (Wipf & Stock, 1987), 182.
44 Greg Brothers, "Patrons and Patronage in the Early Christian Church" *Ministry: International Journal of Pastors*, (July 2002): 12–14, https://www.ministrymagazine.org/archive/2002/07/patrons-and-patronage-in-the-early-christian-church.html.
45 Brown, *Through the Eye of a Needle*, 530.
46 August Turak, *Business Secrets of the Trappist Monks: One CEO's Quest for Meaning and Authenticity* (Columbia Business School Publishing, 2015), 5.
47 Turak, *Business Secrets of the Trappist Monks*, 6.
48 Turak, *Business Secrets of the Trappist Monks*, 6.
49 Turak, *Business Secrets of the Trappist Monks*, 6.
50 Turak, *Business Secrets of the Trappist Monks*, 7.
51 Diarmaid MacCulloch, *Christianity: The First Three Thousand Years* (Penguin, 2010), 369.
52 David Masci, "Key Facts about Government-Favored Religion Around the World," Pew Research Center, October 3, 2017, https://www.pewresearch.org/short-reads/2017/10/03/key-facts-about-government-favored-religion-around-the-world/.
53 George A. Salstrand, *The Story of Stewardship in the United States of America* (Baker, 1956), 31.
54 John H. Reumann, *Stewardship & the Economy of God* (Wipf & Stock, 1992), 54.
55 Henry Lansdell, *The Sacred Tenth or Studies in Tithe-Giving Ancient and Modern* (Baker, 1954).
56 Salstrand, *The Story of Stewardship*, 44.
57 Salstrand, *The Story of Stewardship*, 95, 101, 103, 106, 109, 113, 115, 119, 121.
58 Lindsay, "Pretty Scary."
59 Samuel Lee, *Faith in the Marketplace: Measuring the Impact of Church Based Entrepreneurial Approaches to Holistic Mission* (Pickwick, 2021), 5.

60 Ronald J. Sider, *Churches That Make a Difference: Reaching Your Community with Good News and Good Works* (Baker, 2002), quoted in Lee, *Faith in the Marketplace*, 64.
61 John W. Creswell, *Research Design: Qualitative, Quantitative and Mixed Methods Approaches* (SAGE, 2014), quoted in Lee, 14.
62 Lee, *Faith in the Marketplace*, 84.
63 Lee, *Faith in the Marketplace*, 64.
64 Lee, *Faith in the Marketplace*, 64.
65 Lee, *Faith in the Marketplace*, 64.
66 Lee, *Faith in the Marketplace*, 66.
67 Lee, *Faith in the Marketplace*, 72.
68 Lee, *Faith in the Marketplace*, 76.
69 Lee, *Faith in the Marketplace*, 77.
70 Lee, *Faith in the Marketplace*, 79.
71 Lee, *Faith in the Marketplace*, 80–81.
72 Lee, *Faith in the Marketplace*, 79.
73 Lee, *Faith in the Marketplace*, 80–81.
74 Lee, *Faith in the Marketplace*, 88.
75 Lee, *Faith in the Marketplace*, 107.
76 Lee, *Faith in the Marketplace*, 102.
77 Lee, *Faith in the Marketplace*, 100.
78 Lee, *Faith in the Marketplace*, 100.
79 Lee, *Faith in the Marketplace*, 125.
80 Lee, *Faith in the Marketplace*, 110.
81 Lee, *Faith in the Marketplace*, 122.
82 Lee, *Faith in the Marketplace*, 122.
83 Lee, *Faith in the Marketplace*, 160.
84 Elsdon, *We Aren't Broke*, 8.
85 Elsdon, *We Aren't Broke*, 8n4.
86 Elsdon, *We Aren't Broke*, 8n4.
87 Elsdon, *We Aren't Broke*, xii.
88 Elsdon, *We Aren't Broke*, 108.
89 Elsdon, *We Aren't Broke*, 110.
90 Elsdon, *We Aren't Broke*, 113.
91 Elsdon, *We Aren't Broke*, 123.
92 Elsdon, *We Aren't Broke*, 129.
93 Kretzmann and McKnight, *Building Communities from the Inside Out*, 1.
94 Kretzmann and McKnight, *Building Communities from the Inside Out*, 5.
95 Kretzmann and McKnight, *Building Communities from the Inside Out*, 5.
96 Kretzmann and McKnight, *Building Communities from the Inside Out*, 6.
97 Kretzmann and McKnight, *Building Communities from the Inside Out*, 9.
98 Kretzmann and McKnight, *Building Communities from the Inside Out*, 9.
99 Kretzmann and McKnight, *Building Communities from the Inside Out*, 9.

100 Kretzmann and McKnight, *Building Communities from the Inside Out*, 109.
101 Kretzmann and McKnight, *Building Communities from the Inside Out*, 111.
102 Kretzmann and McKnight, *Building Communities from the Inside Out*, 144–45.
103 Kretzmann and McKnight, *Building Communities from the Inside Out*, 172.
104 Frantz Fanon, *Black Skin, White Masks*, rev. ed. (Grove Press, 2008), 10–12.
105 Mignolo, "Delinking," 333.
106 Mignolo, "Delinking," 333.
107 Stephen Timothy Lenik, "Frontier Landscapes, Missions and Power: A French Jesuit Plantation and Church at Grand Bay, Dominica (1747–1763)" (PhD diss., Syracuse University, 2010), 77–78.
108 "History: Slavery, Memory, and Reconciliation at GU," Georgetown University, accessed October 13, 2025, https://www.georgetown.edu/slavery/history/.
109 Noel Titus, "Concurrence Without Compliance: SPG and the Barbadian Plantations, 1710–1834," in *Three Centuries of Mission: The United Society for the Propagation of the Gospel, 1701–2000*, ed. Daniel O'Connor (Continuum, 2000), 249, 255.
110 Christine J. Hong, *Decolonial Futures: Intercultural and Interreligious Intelligence for Theological Education* (Lexington Books, 2021), 31.
111 Hong, *Decolonial Futures*, 49.
112 Hong, *Decolonial Futures*, 53.
113 Hong, *Decolonial Futures*, 77.
114 Hong, *Decolonial Futures*, 111.
115 Hong, *Decolonial Futures*, 113.
116 Lartey, *Postcolonializing God*, ix.
117 Lartey, *Postcolonializing God*, xvi.
118 Lartey, *Postcolonializing God*, xvi.
119 Lartey, *Postcolonializing God*, xvii.
120 Lartey, *Postcolonializing God*, xvii.
121 Lartey, *Postcolonializing God*, xvii.
122 Lartey, *Postcolonializing God*, xvii.
123 Lartey, *Postcolonializing God*, xviii.
124 Lartey, *Postcolonializing God*, xviii.
125 Lartey, *Postcolonializing God*, 127.
126 Lartey, *Postcolonializing God*, xiii.
127 Hong, *Decolonial Futures*, 165.
128 Hong, *Decolonial Futures*, 171.
129 Dwight J. Zscheile, *The Agile Church: Spirit-Led Innovation in an Uncertain Age* (Morehouse, 2014), 9.

130 Zscheile, *The Agile Church*, 9.
131 Zscheile, *The Agile Church*, 9.
132 Zscheile, *The Agile Church*, 10.
133 Zscheile, *The Agile Church*, 10.
134 Walter Wink, *Naming the Powers: The Language of Power in the New Testament* (Fortress, 1986), 33–34, quoted in Elizabeth Liebert, *The Soul of Discernment: A Spiritual Practice for Communities and Institutions* (Westminster John Knox Press, 2015), 36.
135 Liebert, *The Soul of Discernment*, 37.
136 Liebert, *The Soul of Discernment*, 46.
137 John Cleghorn, *Resurrecting Church: Where Justice and Diversity Meet Radical Welcome and Healing Hope* (Fortress, 2021), 19.
138 Liebert, *The Soul of Discernment*, 78.
139 Liebert, *The Soul of Discernment*, 79.
140 Liebert, *The Soul of Discernment*, 94.
141 Liebert, *The Soul of Discernment*, 94.
142 Liebert, *The Soul of Discernment*, 94.
143 Liebert, *The Soul of Discernment*, 143–45.
144 Liebert, *The Soul of Discernment*, 143.
145 Liebert, *The Soul of Discernment*, 143.
146 Liebert, *The Soul of Discernment*, 144.
147 Zygmunt Bauman, *Wasted Lives: Modernity and its Outcasts* (Polity Press, 2004), 16.
148 Bauman, *Wasted Lives*, 16.
149 Imani Perry, *Vexy Thing: On Gender and Liberation* (Duke University Press, 2018), 102.
150 Bauman, *Wasted Lives*, 82.
151 Judith Butler, "Rethinking Vulnerability and Resistance," in *Vulnerability in Resistance*, eds. Judith Butler, Zeynep Gambetti, and Leticia Sabsay (Duke University Press, 2016), 19.
152 Judith Butler, "Can the Vulnerable Use Their Vulnerability as an Agent of Change?" virtual lecture, February 6, 2015, posted March 6, 2015, by University College Dublin, https://www.youtube.com/watch?v=vwLLElRWp4M; see also Judith Butler, *The Force of Nonviolence: An Ethnic-Political Bind* (Verso, 2020), 197.
153 Perry, *Vexy Thing*, 104.
154 Liebert, *The Soul of Discernment*, 144.
155 Bruno Dyck, "Organization and Management," in *The Routledge Handbook of Economic Theology*, ed. Stefan Schwarzkopf (Routledge, 2020), 201.
156 Dyck, "Organization and Management," 201.
157 Perry, *Vexy Thing*, 21.
158 Neferti X. M. Tadiar, *Remaindered Life* (Duke University Press, 2022), 40.
159 Tadiar, *Remaindered Life*, 45.

160 Bauman, *Wasted Lives*, 46.
161 Audre Lorde, "The Master's Tools Will Never Dismantle the Master's House," in *Sister Outsider: Essays and Speeches* (Crossing Press, 1984), 113.
162 Lorde, "The Master's Tools," 113.
163 Perry, *Vexy Thing*, 34.
164 Bauman, *Wasted Lives*, 66.
165 Tadiar, *Remaindered Life*, 47.
166 Beverly Wildung Harrison, *Justice in the Making: Feminist Social Ethics*, ed. Elizabeth M. Bounds et al. (Westminster John Knox Press, 2004), 183.
167 Perry, *Vexy Thing*, 111.
168 Bauman, *Wasted Lives*, 70.
169 Bauman, *Wasted Lives*, 39.
170 Bauman, *Wasted Lives*, 40.
171 Bauman, *Wasted Lives*, 71.
172 Bruce R. Hopkins and Virginia C. Gross, "Nonprofit Law," in *Nonprofit Management 101: A Complete and Practical Guide for Leaders and Professionals*, 2nd ed., ed. Darian Rodriguez Heyman and Laila Brenner (Wiley & Sons, 2019), 170.
173 Pamela Davis, "Risk Management and Insurance," in Heyman and Brenner, *Nonprofit Management 10l*, 117.
174 Davis, "Risk Management and Insurance," 113.
175 Cassie Scarano and James Weinberg, "Attracting and Hiring Staff: Acquiring the Best Talent" in Heyman and Brenner, *Nonprofit Management 101*, 127.
176 Ronald Kraybill, Robert Evans, and Alice Frazer Evans, *Peace Skills: A Manual for Community Mediators* (Jossey-Bass, 2001), 88.
177 Kretzmann and McKnight, *Building Communities from the Inside Out*, 1, 5.

CHAPTER 2: CASE STUDIES

1 John W. Creswell, *Qualitative Inquiry & Research Design: Choosing Among Five Approaches*, 3rd ed. (SAGE, 2013), 97, 123, 148–49.
2 Ricard Delgado and Jean Stefancic, *Critical Race Theory: An Introduction*, 4th ed. (New York University Press, 2023), 26.
3 Poling and Miller, *Foundations*, 73.
4 Poling and Miller, *Foundations*, 75–76.
5 Michael D. Smith and Jim Waldo, "Anonymity, De-Identification, and the Accuracy of Data," Harvard Online, August 28, 2023, https://www.harvardonline.harvard.edu/blog/anonymity-de-identification-accuracy-data.
6 "Explore Your Neighborhood," the Episcopal Church, accessed September 26, 2024. https://generalconvention.org/explore-your-neighborhood/.
7 The Rev. Barry Randolph, interview by the author, June 30, 2024.
8 "History of the Parish," Cathedral Church of St. Paul, accessed September 26, 2024, https://detroitcathedral.org/our-history/.

9 "History of the Church of the Messiah," Church of the Messiah, https://churchofthemessiahdetroit.org/about/, accessed March 10, 2023. "Church of the Messiah records, 1875–1998," ArchiveGrid, https://researchworks.oclc.org/archivegrid/collection/data/84076792, accessed September 26, 2024.
10 "History of the Church of the Messiah," Church of the Messiah.
11 Randolph, interview, March 10, 2023.
12 The Rev. Wallace Gilbert, Jr., interview by the author, March 21, 2023.
13 Randolph, interview, March 10, 2023.
14 Gilbert, interview, March 21, 2023.
15 David E. Kresta, *Jesus on Main Street: Good News Through Community Economic Development* (Cascade Books, 2021), 122.
16 Mihailo Temali, *Community Economic Development Handbook: Strategies and Tools to Revitalize Your Neighborhood* (Fieldstone Alliance, 2002), 31.
17 Temali, *Community Economic Development Handbook*, 31.
18 Gilbert, interview, March 21, 2023.
19 Tamika Hamilton, interview by the author, February 21, 2023.
20 Gilbert, interview, March 21, 2023.
21 "Equitable Internet Initiative," Detroit Community Technology Project, accessed September 26, 2024, https://tinyurl.com/26zjjyv9.
22 Randolph, interview, March 10, 2023.
23 Randolph, interview, June 30, 2024.
24 Randolph, interview, June 30, 2024.
25 Randolph, interview, March 10, 2023.
26 "Nikki, Ginger and the Tea," *One Detroit*, Detroit Public TV, February 13, 2020, https://www.detroitpbs.org/news-media/one-detroit/nikki-ginger-and-the-tea/?referrer=onedetroitpbs.
27 "Nikki, Ginger and the Tea," *One Detroit*, Detroit Public TV, February 13, 2020.
28 Randolph, interview, June 30, 2024.
29 Randolph, interview, June 30, 2024.
30 Parish focus group, interview by author, Church of the Messiah, June 30, 2024.
31 Gilbert, interview, March 21, 2023.
32 The Rev. Wallace Gilbert, Jr., interview by author, June 30, 2024.
33 "Equitable Internet Initiative," Detroit Community Technology Project.
34 Aaron M. Hill, "How Much Does the Average Church Spend on Payroll?" *ChurchSalary*, July 25, 2022. https://www.churchsalary.com/content/articles/how-much-of-budget-do-churches-spend-on-salaries-payroll.html.
35 Randolph, interview, March 10, 2023.
36 Cleghorn, *Resurrecting Church*, 47.
37 Randolph, interview, March 10, 2023.
38 Angie Jackson, "A Church-Run Business Incubator Grows Its Community's Own Solutions to Poverty," Faith and Leadership, September 1, 2020, https://tinyurl.com/4rszexzf.

39 Randolph, interview, March 10, 2023.
40 Gilbert, interview, March 21, 2023.
41 Randolph, interview, June 30, 2024.
42 Parishioner focus group interview by the author, Church of the Messiah, June 30, 2024.
43 Cleghorn, *Resurrecting Church*, 19.
44 Liebert, *The Soul of Discernment*, 78.
45 Parishioner focus group, interview, June 30, 2024.
46 Randolph, interview, March 10, 2023.
47 Randolph, interview, March 10, 2023.
48 Hamilton, interview, February 21, 2023.
49 Randolph, interview, June 30, 2024.
50 Randolph, interview, March 10, 2023.
51 Gilbert, interview, March 21, 2023.
52 Randolph, interview, March 10, 2023.
53 Randolph, interview, March 10, 2023.
54 Randolph, interview, March 10, 2023.
55 Parishioner focus group, interview, June 30, 2024.
56 Hamilton, interview, February 21, 2023.
57 Parishioner focus group, interview, June 30, 2024.
58 Kresta, *Jesus on Main Street*, 163.
59 Kresta, *Jesus on Main Street*, 163.
60 Kresta, *Jesus on Main Street*, 164.
61 Randolph, interview, March 10, 2023.
62 Randolph, interview, March 10, 2023.
63 Cleghorn, *Resurrecting Church*, 10.
64 Cleghorn, *Resurrecting Church*, 11.
65 Heidi M. Neck, Christopher P. Neck, and Emma L. Murray, *Entrepreneurship: The Practice and Mindset* (SAGE, 2018), 9.
66 Cleghorn, *Resurrecting Church*, 19.
67 Cleghorn, *Resurrecting Church*, 105.
68 Kresta, *Jesus on Main Street*, 18–22.
69 The Rev. Jamesetta Ferguson, interview by the author, June 12, 2023.
70 The Rev. Jamesetta Ferguson, interview by the author, June 25, 2024.
71 Katherine Schaeffer, "Key Facts About Housing Affordability in the U.S." Pew Research Center, March 23, 2022, https://tinyurl.com/42ehnw3m.
72 "Explore Your Neighborhood," the Episcopal Church.
73 The Rev. Jamesetta Ferguson, interview by the author, July 12, 2024.
74 Ferguson, interview, June 12, 2023.
75 Hans Holznagel, "Small Louisville Church Creatively Raises $7M to Return Hope to Urban Neighborhood," *United Church of Christ News*, March 12, 2020, https://www.ucc.org/small_louisville_church_creatively_raises_7m_to_return_hope_to_urban_neighborhood/.

76 Kate Eller, "Norton Healthcare Announces Permanent Location for its Institute for Health Equity," Norton Healthcare, March 10, 2023, https://nortonhealthcare.com/news/norton-healthcare-announces-permanent-location-for-its-institute-for-health-equity/.
77 "Health Equity Means Giving Every Person in Every Community the Same Access to Care and Opportunity to Be as Healthy as Possible, No Matter Their Race, Gender or Any Other Influence on Their Life," Norton Healthcare, May 31, 2023, https://nortonhealthcare.com/news/breaking-down-barriers-to-health-equity/.
78 Ferguson, interview, June 25, 2024.
79 Hans Holznagel, "As MOLO Opening Nears, Tenants 'Thank God' for Louisville Pastor's Vision," *United Church of Christ News*, March 11, 2021, https://www.ucc.org/as-molo-opening-nears-tenants-thank-god-for-louisville-pastors-vision/.
80 Holznagel, "As MOLO Opening Nears."
81 Holznagel, "As MOLO Opening Nears."
82 Holznagel, "As MOLO Opening Nears."
83 "Welcome to Amped," Amped Louisville, accessed September 26, 2024, https://ampedlouisville.org/.
84 Ferguson, interview, June 12, 2023.
85 Ferguson, interview, June 12, 2023.
86 Ferguson, interview, June 12, 2023.
87 Ferguson, interview, June 12, 2023.
88 Ferguson, interview, April 12, 2023.
89 Hans Holznagel, "UCC Film About Project in Urban Neighborhood Wins UN Festival Honor," United Church of Christ, July 27, 2022. https://www.ucc.org/ucc-film-about-project-in-urban-neighborhood-wins-un-festival-honor/.
90 Holznagel, "UCC Film."
91 Holznagel, "UCC Film."
92 Holznagel, "UCC Film."
93 Holznagel, "Small Louisville Church Creatively Raises $7M."
94 "Historic West Louisville Church to Receive $2 Million Expansion Project," WDRB.com, December 19, 2022. https://www.wdrb.com/news/business/historic-west-louisville-church-to-receive-2-million-expansion-project/article_52e73262-7fdb-11ed-a64b-1faafa458967.html.
95 Ferguson, interview, June 12, 2023.
96 Holznagel, "Small Louisville Church Creatively Raises $7M."
97 Ferguson, interview, June 12, 2023.
98 Speech by the Rev. Dr. Patrick Duggan, Neighborhood Economics Conference, Portland, OR, January 30, 2023.
99 Ferguson, interview, June 12, 2023.
100 Ferguson, interview, June 12, 2023.
101 Ferguson, interview, June 12, 2023.

102 Holznagel, "UCC Film."
103 Jay Tennier, "Rev. Jamesetta Ferguson, Daily Point of Light #4246," *Points of Light*, May 17, 2010. https://www.pointsoflight.org/awards/rev-jamesetta-ferguson/.
104 Kresta, *Jesus on Main Street*, 163.
105 Meghan Sobocienski, Grace in Action Collectives, and Pastor John Cummins, Grace in Action Church, interviews by Collaborative Inquiry Team, October 6, 2020, YouTube, by Southeast Center for Cooperative Development, October 9, 2020, https://www.youtube.com/watch?v=gTq_nhQxPAs&t=5s.
106 Tadiar, *Remaindered Life*, 114.
107 "Explore Your Neighborhood," the Episcopal Church, ArcGIS online, accessed September 26, 2024, https://dfms-tec.maps.arcgis.com/apps/mapviewer/index.html?webmap=5dc50120ce354313959aeab3355f7148.
108 "Explore Your Neighborhood," the Episcopal Church.
109 "Explore Your Neighborhood," the Episcopal Church.
110 "Explore Your Neighborhood," the Episcopal Church, https://dfms-tec.maps.arcgis.com/apps/mapviewer/index.html?webmap=963f56c39d654c2084275d8f51fe12fe.
111 "Explore Your Neighborhood," the Episcopal Church, https://dfms-tec.maps.arcgis.com/apps/mapviewer/index.html?webmap=ab1547245f2e42c999042ba13fae55e1.
112 Magid Shihade, "Asabiyya," in *Changing Theory: Concepts from the Global South*, ed. Dilip M. Menon (Routledge, 2022), 176.
113 Shihade, "Asabiyaa," 176.
114 Shihade, "Asabiyaa," 178.
115 Pastor John Cummins, Grace in Action Church, interview by the author, October 19, 2023.
116 Cummins, interview, October 19, 2023.
117 Cummins, interview, October 19, 2023.
118 Cummins, interview, October 19, 2023.
119 Southeast Center for Cooperative Development, Recorded Interview with Sobocienski and Cummins, Collaborative Inquiry Team, October 6, 2020.
120 Cummins, interview, October 19, 2023.
121 Lynn Pitman, "History of Cooperatives in the United States: An Overview," Center for Cooperatives, University of Wisconsin-Madison, December 2018, https://resources.uwcc.wisc.edu/History_of_Cooperatives.pdf.
122 John Raymaker and Pierre Whalon, *Attentive, Intelligent, Rational, and Responsible: Transforming Economics to Save the Planet* (Marquette University Press, 2023), 112.
123 John S. Moolakkattu, "Mahatma Gandhi and the Environment," The Energy and Resources Institute, October 1, 2019. https://www.teriin.org/article/mahatma-gandhi-and-environment.

124 Bauman, *Wasted Lives*, 72; Maria Mies, *Patriarchy and Accumulation on a World Scale: Women in the International Division of Labor* (Bloomsbury, 1986), 217.
125 Bauman, *Wasted Lives*, 20.
126 Bauman, *Wasted Lives*, 20.
127 Bauman, *Wasted Lives*, 16.
128 Southeast Center for Cooperative Development, Recorded Interview with Sobocienski and Cummins, Collaborative Inquiry Team, October 6, 2020.
129 Southeast Center for Cooperative Development, Recorded Interview with Sobocienski and Cummins, Collaborative Inquiry Team, October 6, 2020.
130 Cummins, interview, October 19, 2023.
131 Bauman, *Wasted Lives*, 92–93.
132 Perry, *Vexy Thing: On Gender and Liberation*, 104.
133 Tadiar, *Remaindered Life*, 45.
134 Bauman, *Wasted Lives*, 66.
135 Bauman, *Wasted Lives*, 70.
136 Gil Rendle, *Countercultural: Subversive Resistance and the Neighborhood Congregation* (Rowman and Littlefield, 2023), 32–36.
137 Rendle, *Countercultural*, 116.
138 Rendle, *Countercultural*, 137.
139 Rendle, *Countercultural*, 148.
140 Cummins, interview, October 19, 2023.
141 Cummins, interview, October 19, 2023.
142 "City and Town Population Totals: 2020–2023," US Census Bureau, https://www.census.gov/data/tables/time-series/demo/popest/2020s-total-cities-and-towns.html.
143 "2020 Census Demographic Data Map Viewer," US Census Bureau, https://www.census.gov/library/visualizations/2021/geo/demographicmapviewer.html.
144 "Quick Facts: Fall River, Massachusetts; United States," US Census Bureau, https://www.census.gov/quickfacts/fact/table/fallrivercitymassachusetts,US/PST04219.
145 "Fast Facts," University of Massachusetts Dartmouth, accessed May 15, 2025, https://www.umassd.edu/undergraduate/facts/.
146 The Rev. Scott A. Ciosek, interview with the author, May 8, 2024.
147 "Explore Your Neighborhood," the Episcopal Church.
148 "Explore Your Neighborhood," the Episcopal Church.
149 "A Brief History of St. Peter's," St. Peter's Episcopal Church, accessed April 26, 2025, https://stpetersdartmouth.org/new/.
150 The Rev. Scott A. Ciosek, interview with the author, August 5, 2024.
151 Ciosek, interview, August 5, 2024.
152 Ciosek, interview, August 5, 2024.
153 Ciosek, interview, August 5, 2024.
154 Ciosek, interview, August 5, 2024.

155 Ciosek, interview, August 5, 2024.
156 "Our Team," The Bridge: A Center for Hope and Healing, https://thebridgedartmouth.org/our-team/.
157 Ciosek, interview, May 4, 2024.
158 Ciosek, interview, May 4, 2024.
159 "Explore Individual Parochial Report Trends," the General Convention of the Episcopal Church, Episcopal Church Research and Statistics, accessed October 14, 2024, https://generalconvention.org/explore-parochial-report-trends/.
160 Cleghorn, *Resurrecting Church*, 19.
161 Liebert, *The Soul of Discernment*, 78.
162 Ciosek, interview, May 8, 2024.
163 Kresta, *Jesus on Main Street*, 18–22.

CHAPTER 3: QUANTITATIVE DATA

1 Roger Tourangeau, "Survey Reliability: Models, Methods, and Findings," *Journal of Survey Statistics and Methodology* 9, no. 5 (November 2021): 961–91, https://www.ncbi.nlm.nih.gov/pmc/articles/PMC8665769/.

CHAPTER 4: BEST PRACTICES AND PRACTICAL THEOLOGY

1 Lorde, "The Master's Tools," 113.
2 Poling and Miller, *Foundations*, 61, 169.

POSTLUDE

1 Liebert, *Soul of Discernment*, 42.
2 Ronald Kraybill, Robert Evans, Alice Frazer Evans, *Peace Skills*, 68.
3 Stephen Lewis, Matthew Wesley Williams, and Dori Grinenko Baker, *Another Way: Living and Leading Change on Purpose* (Chalice Press, 2020), 59.
4 Lewis, Williams, and Baker, *Another Way*, 111.
5 Lisa Esposito, "Respite Care: Giving Caregivers a Break," *U.S. News & World Report*, April 13, 2022.
6 Esposito, "Respite Care."
7 Esposito, "Respite Care."
8 Esposito, "Respite Care."
9 Esposito, "Respite Care."
10 "Adult Day Services Centers," Centers for Disease Control and Prevention, last reviewed December 19, 2024, https://www.cdc.gov/nchs/fastats/adsc.htm.

11 "Adult Day Services Centers," Centers for Disease Control and Prevention, https://www.cdc.gov/nchs/fastats/adsc.htm.
12 Vincent Rome, Jessica Penn Lendon, and Lauren Harris-Kojetin, "Differences in Characteristics of Adult Day Services Centers, by Level of Medical Service Provision," National Center for Health Statistics, *Vital and Health Statistics*, Series 3, Number 45, October 2020, 6, https://stacks.cdc.gov/view/cdc/96032
13 Vincent Rome, Jessica Penn Lendon, Lauren Harris-Kojetin, "Differences in Characteristics of Adult Day Services Centers," 8.
14 Liebert, *Soul of Discernment*, 19.
15 Liebert, *Soul of Discernment*, 21.

Bibliography

Barna Group. *Church Startups and Money: The Myths and Realities of Church Planxters and Finances.* Barna Group, 2016.

Barnes, Kenneth J. *Redeeming Capitalism.* Eerdmans, 2018.

Bauman, Zygmunt. *Wasted Lives: Modernity and Its Outcasts.* Polity Press, 2004.

Benac, Dustin D. *Adaptive Church: Collaboration and Community in a Changing World.* Baylor University Press, 2022.

Bowler, Kate. *Blessed: A History of the American Prosperity Gospel.* Oxford University Press, 2018.

Brown, Peter. *Through the Eye of a Needle: Wealth, the Fall of Rome, and the Making of Christianity in the West, 350–550 AD.* Princeton University Press, 2012.

Brueggemann, Walter. *The Creative Word: Canon as a Model for Biblical Education.* Fortress Press, 2015.

Brueggemann, Walter. *Money and Possessions.* Westminster John Knox Press, 2016.

Butler, Judith. "Rethinking Vulnerability and Resistance." In *Vulnerability in Resistance*, edited by Judith Butler, Zeynep Gambetti, and Leticia Sabsay, 12–27. Duke University Press, 2016.

Butler, Judith, Zeynep Gambetti, and Leticia Sabsay, eds. *Vulnerability in Resistance.* Duke University Press, 2016.

Cavanagh, John and Jerry Mander, eds. *Alternatives to Economic Globalization: A Better World Is Possible.* 2nd ed. Berrett-Koehler Publishers, 2004.

Cavanaugh, William T. *Being Consumed: Economics and Christian Desire.* Eerdmans, 2008.

Chilcote, Paul Wesley, annot. *John & Charles Wesley: Selections from Their Writings and Hymns—Annotated & Explained.* Skylight Paths Publishing, 2011.

Chung-Kim, Esther and Todd R. Hains. *Reformation Commentary on Scripture: Acts.* IVP Academic, 2014.

Cleghorn, John. *Resurrecting Church: Where Justice and Diversity Meet Radical Welcome and Healing Hope.* Fortress, 2021.

Commins, Gary. *Evil and The Problem of Jesus.* Cascade Books, 2023.

Cox, Harvey. *The Market as God.* Harvard University Press, 2016.

Creswell, John W. *Qualitative Inquiry & Research Design: Choosing Among Five Approaches*. 3rd ed. Sage, 2013.

Daly, Herman F. and John B. Cobb, Jr. *For the Common Good: Redirecting the Economy Toward Community, the Environment and a Sustainable Future*. Rev. ed. Beacon Press, 1994.

Davis, Pamela. "Risk Management and Insurance." In *Nonprofit Management 101: A Complete and Practical Guide for Leaders and Professionals*. 2nd ed., edited by Darian Rodriguez Heyman and Laila Brenner, 107–119. John Wiley & Sons, 2019.

Delgado, Richard, and Jean Stefancic. *Critical Race Theory: An Introduction*, 4th ed. New York University Press, 2023.

Deymaz, Mark, and Harry Li. *The Coming Revolution in Church Economics: Why Tithes and Offerings Are No Longer Enough, and What You Can Do About It*. Baker, 2019.

Drake, Janine Giordano. *The Gospel of Church: How Mainline Protestants Vilified Christian Socialism and Fractured the Labor Movement*. Oxford University Press, 2024.

Duggan, Rev. Dr. Patrick. Speech at the Neighborhood Economics Conference. Portland, OR, January 30, 2023.

Dyck, Bruno. "Organization and Management." In *The Routledge Handbook of Economic Theology*, edited by Stefan Schwarzkopf. Routledge, 2020.

Eale Bosela E., and Njoroge J. Ngige. *Complexities of Theologies of Wealth and Prosperity: Africa in Focus*. Regnum Books, 2022.

Ellacuría, Ignacio. *Ignacio Ellacuría: Essays on History, Liberation and Salvation*. Edited and translated by Micheal E. Lee. Orbis, 2013.

Elsdon, Mark. *We Aren't Broke: Uncovering Hidden Resources for Mission and Ministry*. Eerdmans, 2021.

Elsdon, Mark. *Gone for Good? Negotiating the Coming Wave of Church Property Transition*. Eerdmans, 2024.

Emmett, Ross B. "The Entrepreneur." In Schwarzkopf, *Routledge Handbook*.

Esposito, Lisa. "Respite Care: Giving Caregivers a Break." *U.S. News & World Report*. April 13, 2022.

Fahmy, Dalia. "European Countries That Have Mandatory Church Taxes Are About as Religious as Their neighbors That Don't." Pew Research Center, May 9, 2019. https://www.pewresearch.org/short-reads/2019/05/09/european-countries-that-have-mandatory-church-taxes-are-about-as-religious-as-their-neighbors-that-dont/.

Fascar, Fanny. "The Nigerian Megachurches' Business with Faith." *DW*. September 18, 2018. https://www.dw.com/en/nigerian-pentecostal-megachurches-a-booming-business/a-45535263.

Foster, John Bellamy. "Marxism and Ecology: Common Fonts of a Great Tradition," *Monthly Review* 67, no. 7 (December 2015): 1–13. https://monthlyreview.org/2015/12/01/marxism-and-ecology/.

Fraser Nancy and Rahel Jaeggi. *Capitalism: A Conversation in Critical Theory.* Verso, 2023.

Friedman, Benjamin M. *Religion and the Rise of Capitalism.* Vantage Books, 2022.

González, Justo. *Faith and Wealth: A History of Early Christian Ideas on the Origin, Significance and Use of Money.* Wipf & Stock, 1990.

Griffin, David Ray, John Cobb, Richard Falk, and Catherine Keller. *The American Empire and the Commonwealth of God: A Political, Economic, Religious Statement.* Westminster John Knox Press. 2006.

Harrison, Beverly Wildung. *Justice in the Making: Feminist Social Ethics,* edited by Elizabeth M. Bounds, Pamela K. Brubaker, Jane E. Hicks, Marilyn J. Legge, Rebecca Todd Peters, and Traci C. West. Westminster John Knox Press, 2004.

Harvey, David. *The Limits to Capital.* Verso, 2018.

Henkel-Rieger, Rosemarie. "Deep Solidarity: A Pre-requisite to Resisting Capitalism and Building Economic Democracy." In *Faith, Class & Labor: Intersectional Approaches in a Global Context,* edited by Jin Young Choi and Joerg Rieger. Pickwick.

Heyman, Darian and Laila Brenner. *Nonprofit Management 101: A Complete and Practical Guide for Leaders and Professionals,* 2nd ed. John Wiley & Sons, 2019.

Heyward, Carter. *The Seven Deadly Sins of White Christian Nationalism: A Call to Action.* Rowman & Littlefield, 2022.

Hinze, Christine Firer. "What is Enough?" In *Having: Property and Possession in Religious and Social Life.* Edited by William Schweiker and Charles Mathewes. Eerdmans, 2004.

Hirschfeld, Mary L. *Aquinas and the Market: Toward a Humane Economy.* Harvard University Press, 2018.

Hong, Christine J. *Decolonial Futures: Intercultural and Interreligious Intelligence for Theological Education.* Lexington Books, 2021.

Hopkins, Bruce R. and Virginia C. Gross. "Nonprofit Law." In Heyman and Brenner, *Nonprofit Management 101: A Complete and Practical Guide for Leaders and Professionals.*

John Paul II. "Work as a Sharing in the Activity of the Creator." In *Laborem Exercens* (Through Work). September 14, 1981. https://www.vatican.va/content/john-paul-ii/en/encyclicals/documents/hf_jp-ii_enc_14091981_laborem-exercens.html.

Johnson, C. Neal. *Business as Mission: A Comprehensive Guide to Theory and Practice.* IVP Academic, 2011.

Johnson, Luke Timothy. *Sharing Possessions: What Faith Demands.* 2nd ed. Eerdmans, 2011.

Johnston, Carol. *The Wealth or Health of Nations: Transforming Capitalism from Within.* The Pilgrim Press, 1998.

Kendall, R.T. *Tithing: Discover the Freedom of Biblical Giving*. Zondervan, 1982.

Keucher, Gerald W. *Remember the Future: Financial Leadership and Asset Management for Congregations*. Church Publishing, 2006.

Kitawi, Caroline Njambi, and Dancan Njagi Irungu. "How Church-Owned Businesses Promote Sustainability of the Church: A Case of Selected Churches in Nairobi Kenya." *International Journal of Economics, Commerce and Management* 3, no. 6 (June 2015): 1025–1037. https://ijecm.co.uk/wp-content/uploads/2015/06/3663.pdf.

Kraybill, Ronald, Robert Evans, and Alice Frazer Evans. *Peace Skills: A Manual for Community Mediators*. Jossey-Bass, 2001.

Kresta, David E. *Jesus on Main Street: Good News Through Community Economic Development*. Cascade Books, 2021.

Kretzmann, John P. and John L. McKnight. *Building Communities from the Inside Out: A Path Toward Finding and Mobilizing a Community's Assets*. Acta Publications, 1993.

Lansdell, Henry. *The Sacred Tenth or Studies in Tithe-Giving Ancient and Modern*. Baker, 1954.

Lartey, Emmanuel Y. *Postcolonializing God: An African Practical Theology*. SMC Press, 2013.

Lee, Samuel. *Faith in the Marketplace: Measuring the Impact of Church Based Entrepreneurial Approaches to Holistic Mission*. Pickwick, 2021.

Lenik, Stephen Timothy. "Frontier Landscapes, Missions and Power: A French Jesuit Plantation and Church at Grand Bay, Dominica (1747–1763)." PhD diss., Syracuse University, 2010.

Lewis, Stephen, Matthew Wesley Williams, and Dori Grinenko Baker. *Another Way: Living and Leading Change on Purpose*. Chalice Press, 2020.

Liebert, Elizabeth. *The Soul of Discernment: A Spiritual Practice for Communities and Institutions*. Westminster John Knox Press, 2015.

Lindsay, Drew. "'Pretty Scary': 7 Things to Know About Religion's Decline and Charitable Giving," *The Chronicle of Philanthropy*, December 12, 2023.

Lorde, Audre. "The Master's Tools Will Never Dismantle the Master's House." In *Sister Outsider: Essays and Speeches*. Crossing Press, 1984.

Lowe, Lisa. *The Intimacies of Four Continents*. Duke University Press, 2015.

Lynn, Andrew. *Saving the Protestant Ethic: Creative Class Evangelism and the Crisis of Work*. Oxford University Press, 2023.

MacCulloch, Diarmaid. *Christianity: The First Three Thousand Years*. Penguin, 2010.

Margolies, Jane. "The Church with the $6 Billion Portfolio," *New York Times*, February 8, 2019. https://www.nytimes.com/2019/02/08/nyregion/trinity-church-manhattan-real-estate.html.

Matz, Brian. "The Principle of Detachment from Private Property in Basil of Caesarea's Homily 6 and Its Context." In *Reading Patristic Texts on Social*

Ethics, edited by Johan Leemans, Brian J. Matz and Johan Verstraeten. Catholic University of America Press, 2011.

McCarraher, Eugene. *The Enchantments of Mammon: How Capitalism Became the Religion of Modernity*. MA: Belknap Press, 2019.

McFague, Sallie. *Life Abundant: Rethinking Theology and Economy for a Planet in Peril*. Fortress, 2000.

Menakem, Resmaa. *My Grandmother's Hands: Radicalized Trauma and the Pathways to Mending Our Hearts and Bodies*. CRP, 2017.

Mies, Maria. *Patriarchy and Accumulation on a World Scale: Women in the International Division of Labor*. Bloomsbury, 1986.

Mignolo, Walter D. "Introduction: Coloniality of Power and De-Colonial Thinking." In *Globalization and the Decolonial Option*, edited by Walter D. Mignolo and Arturo Escobar. Routledge, 2013.

Mignolo, Walter D. "Delinking: The Rhetoric of Modernity, The Logic of Coloniality and The Grammar of De-Coloniality." In *Globalization and the Decolonial Option*.

Moon, W. Jay. *Missional Vibrancy and Financial Viability: Alternative Financial Models for Churches and Church Plants When Tithes and Offerings Are Not Enough*. W. Jay Moon, 2021.

Morales, Dawn A., Crystal L. Barksdale, and Andrea C. Beckel-Mitchener. "A Call to Action to Address Rural Mental Health Disparities." *Journal of Clinical and Translational Science*, 4, no. 5 (2020): 463–467, https://www.doi.org/10.1017/cts.2020.42.

Neal, Jerusha Matsen. "A Question of Consequence." Duke Chapel Sermons. October 1, 2023. https://www.youtube.com/watch?v=7hXGSb92W-k.

Neck, Heidi M., Christopher P. Neck, and Emma L. Murray. *Entrepreneurship: The Practice and Mindset*. SAGE, 2018.

Niebuhr, H. Richard. *The Church against the World*. Willett, Clark, 1935.

Nkamuhabwa Keshomshahara, Abednego. "Positive Relationship between Economics and Theology." In *Complexities of Theology of Wealth and Prosperity: Africa in Focus*, edited by Bosela E. Eale and Njoroge J. Ngige. Regnum, 2022.

Noll, Mark A. *The Old Religion in a New World: The History of North American Christianity*. Eerdmans, 2002.

Novak, Michael. *The Spirit of Democratic Capitalism*. Madison Books, 1982.

Osmer Richard R. *Practical Theology: An Introduction*. Eerdmans, 2008.

Perry, Imani. *Vexy Thing: On Gender and Liberation*. Duke University Press, 2018.

Poling James N. and Donald E. Miller. *Foundations for a Practical Theology of Ministry*. Abingdon, 1985.

Pritchard, Robert W. *A History of the Episcopal Church*. Morehouse, 2014.

Raymaker, John and Pierre Whalon. *Attentive, Intelligent, Rational and Responsible: Transforming Economics to Save the Planet.* Marquette University Press, 2023.

Rendle, Gil. *Countercultural: Subversive Resistance and the Neighborhood Congregation.* Rowman and Littlefield, 2023.

Reumann, John H. *Stewardship & The Economy of God.* Wipf & Stock, 1992.

Rieger, Joerg. *Theology in the Capitalocene: Ecology, Identity, Class and Solidarity.* Fortress, 2022.

Rieger, Joerg. *No Rising Tide: Theology, Economics and the Future.* Fortress, 2009.

Rogers-Vaughn, Bruce. *Caring For Souls in A Neoliberal Age.* Palgrave Macmillan, 2016.

Rohr, Richard. *A Lever & A Place to Stand: The Contemplative Stance, the Active Prayer.* Paulist Press, 2001.

Rome, Vincent, Jessica Penn Lendon, and Lauren Harris-Kojetin. "Differences in Characteristics of Adult Day Services Centers, by Level of Medical Service Provision." National Center for Health Statistics, *Vital and Health Statistics,* Series 3, Number 45, October 2020.

Rothauge, Arlin. "Continuum of Community Involvement and Social Transformation." Unpublished class materials edited by Sheryl Kujawa-Holbrook, 2010.

Sabsay, Leticia. "Vulnerability, Affective Powers, Hegemony." In Butler, Gambetti, and Sabsay, *Vulnerability in Resistance.*

Salstrand, George A. *The Story of Stewardship in the United States of America.* Baker, 1956.

Salter, Alexander William. *The Political Economy of Distribution: Property, Liberty and the Common Good.* Catholic University of America Press, 2023.

Samuel, Frouison. "A Theological Response to the Ecological Crisis, Wealth and Prosperity." In *Complexities of Theologies of Wealth and Prosperity: Africa in Focus.* Edited by Bosela E. Eale and Njoroge J. Ngige. Regnum, 2022.

Scarano, Cassie and James Weinberg. "Attracting and Hiring Staff: Acquiring the Best Talent" in Heyman and Brenner, *Nonprofit Management 101: A Complete and Practical Guide for Leaders and Professionals.* 2nd ed.

Schor, Juliet B. *Plentitude: The New Economics of True Wealth.* Penguin, 2010.

Schor, Juliet B. "What Can We Do About Income Inequality?," Creating the Common Good, January 24, 2015, Trinity Church NYC, https://trinitychurchnyc.org/videos/juliet-schor-keynote.

Schut, Michael. *Money & Faith: The Search for Enough.* Morehouse Publishing, 2008.

Schwarzkopf, Stefan, ed. *The Routledge Handbook of Economic Theology.* Routledge, 2021.

Shihade, Magid. "Asabiyya." In *Changing Theory: Concepts from the Global South*, edited by Dilip M. Menon. Routledge, 2022.

Simpson, Peter. "Leadership." In Schwartzkopf, *Routledge Handbook.*

Singh, Devin. *Divine Currency: The Theological Power of Money in the West.* Stanford University Press, 2018.

Sitze, Bob. *Stewardshift: An Economia for Congregational Change.* Church Publishing, 2016.

Spellers, Stephanie. *The Church Cracked Open.* Church Publishing, 2022.

Sung, Jung Mo. *Desire Market and Religion.* SCM Press, 2007.

Tadiar, Neferti X. M. *Remaindered Life.* Duke University Press, 2022.

Tan, Jonathon W. "Behavioral Economics of Religion." In *The Oxford Handbook of Christianity and Economics*, edited by Paul Oslington. Oxford University Press, 2014.

Tanner, Kathryn, *Economy of Grace.* Fortress, 2005.

Tanner, Kathryn. *Christianity and the New Spirit of Capitalism.* Yale University Press, 2019.

Taylor, Keeanga-Yamahtta. *#Blacklivesmatter to Black Liberation.* Haymarket Books, 2016.

Temali, Mihailo. *Community Economic Development Handbook: Strategies and Tools to Revitalize Your Neighborhood.* Fieldstone Alliance, 2002.

Tertullian. *The Apology in The Ante-Nicene Fathers.* Hendrickson Publishing, 1995. Quoted in Richard Rohr, *A Lever and a Place to Stand: The Contemplative Stance, the Active Prayer.* The Paulist Press, 2001.

Titus, Noel. "Concurrence Without Compliance: SPG and the Barbadian Plantations, 1710–1834." In *Three Centuries of Mission: The United Society for the Propagation of the Gospel, 1701–2000*, edited by Daniel O'Connor. Continuum, 2000.

Tiwari, Rajnarayan R. "Gandhi as an Environmentalist," *Indian Journal of Medical Research* 149 Suppl 1 (January 2019): S142.

Turak, August. *Business Secrets of the Trappist Monks: One CEO's Quest for Meaning and Authenticity.* Columbia Business School Publishing, 2015.

University of Michigan Library. "Church of the Messiah Records, 1875–1998." https://findingaids.lib.umich.edu/catalog/umich-bhl-98116.

Ward, Kate. *Wealth, Virtue, and Moral Luck: Christian Ethics in an Age of Inequality.* Georgetown University Press, 2021.

Wariboko, Nimi. *God and Money: A Theology of Money in a Globalizing World.* Rowman and Littlefield, 2008.

Waters, Brent. *Just Capitalism: A Christian Ethic of Economic Globalization.* Westminster John Knox Press, 2016.

Weber, Max. *The Protestant Ethic and the Spirit of Capitalism.* Charles Scribner's Sons, 1958.

Welby, Justin. *Dethroning Mammon: Making Money Serve Grace.* Bloomsbury, 2016.

Wheeler, Sondra Ely. *Wealth as Peril and Obligation.* Eerdmans, 1995.

White, Lynn Jr. "The Historical Roots of Our Ecological Crisis," *Science* 155 (March 10, 1967), 1203–08.

Wink, Walter. *Naming the Powers: The Language of Power in the New Testament*. Fortress, 1986.

Young, Frances M, and David F. Ford. *Meaning and Truth in Second Corinthians*. Wipf & Stock, 1987.

Zhang, Ning. "A Forgotten History: Marxist Ecology after Marx." *Critical Sociology* 49, no. 1 (January 2023): 165–171. https://doi.org/10.1177/08969205221095273.

Zscheile, Dwight J. *The Agile Church: Spirit-Led Innovation in an Uncertain Age*. Morehouse, 2014.

Index